KINDLING DESIRE FOR GOD

Praise for

KINDLING DESIRE FOR GOD

"Kay Northcutt is a gift—and so is this book. It is not only a joy to read, it is a joy to 'live into.' Her new—and very old—approach to preaching as spiritual direction is one that will help us to become the 'god-persons,' the spokespersons for God that we have been called to be. Good critical reflection and moving vivid imagery help to make this a lovely and most important book for our time."

 —*Joseph R. Jeter, Brite Divinity School*

"Kay Northcutt teaches through word and example how preaching can—and must—cultivate a space to encounter the living God. In the words of George Herbert, one of the many spiritual teachers she draws upon, every word in this book is "heart-deep." An indispensable guide for preachers and a feast for anyone seeking to kindle desire for God."

 —*Stephanie Paulsell, Harvard Divinity School*

"Preachers discover, often to their surprise, that they function as spiritual directors, that their listeners long for a deeper sense of the presence of God in their lives. Professor Northcutt has produced an important resource that will help us reflect on, and grow into, this critical dimension of the life of the church and it ministry."

 —*John M. Buchanan, Pastor, The Fourth Presbyterian Church of*
   Chicago; Editor, The Christian Century

"Kay Northcutt recognizes the need for pastors to attend to their spiritual lives and provides guidance in the ways of renewal."

 —*Rev. Jane E. Vennard, Spiritual Director; Senior Adjunct Faculty,*
   Iliff School of Theology

"I am anxious to see what a church looks like whose preacher adopts this new paradigm."

 —*Fred B. Craddock, from the foreword*

KINDLING DESIRE FOR GOD

PREACHING AS SPIRITUAL DIRECTION

Kay L. Northcutt

Fortress Press
MINNEAPOLIS

For my teachers:

Greg Heille, Jill Clupper, Joe Bessler

KINDLING DESIRE FOR GOD
Preaching as Spiritual Direction

Scripture passages are from the New Revised Standard Version of the Bible © copyright 1989 by the Division of Christian Education of the National Council of the Churches of Christ in the USA. Used by permission. All rights reserved.

Cover image © iStockphoto.com/Amanda Rohde
Cover design: Ivy Palmer Skrade
Book design: Michelle L. N. Cook

Library of Congress Cataloging-in-Publication Data
Northcutt, Kay Bessler, 1957-
  Kindling desire for God: preaching as spiritual direction / Kay L. Northcutt.
    p. cm.
  Includes bibliographical references and index.
  ISBN 978-0-8006-6263-9 (alk. paper)
  1. Preaching. 2. Spiritual direction—Christianity. I. Title.
  BV4211.3.N67 2009
  251–dc22   2008043397

The paper used in this publication meets the minimum requirements of American National Standard for Information Sciences—Permanence of Paper for Printed Library Materials, ANSI Z329.48-1984.

Manufactured in the U.S.A.

CONTENTS

121051

FOREWORD

WHEN FIRST I READ THE TITLE OF THIS BOOK, *Kindling Desire for God,* I chuckled to myself. "The publisher's marketing department had its way again." Marketing departments are not concerned who the readers are as long as there are lots of them. Their job is to get prospective readers to pick up the book; it is the writer's responsibility to keep them reading. Hence the marketer's interest in titles. They will sometimes consent to a subtitle if an author insists on plain honesty about content, as in the present case, *Preaching as Spiritual Direction.* So, I thought, the title attracts everyone, lay and clergy alike, but, in fact, the book is for clergy, and more particularly, clergy who preach.

I could not have been more wrong. Both the title and the subtitle are honest and straightforward because the book is conversation with the whole church about preaching. This is no small achievement. As her primary act, Professor Northcutt relocates the person in the pulpit as a vital component of the preaching event. I say "relocates" for two reasons: one, recent studies in homiletics have tended to neglect the preacher's life and faith and character as ingredient to the speaking-hearing experience. The author is not satisfied simply to repeat Phillips Brooks's famous definition, "Truth through personality." Rather, she redefines the preacher as one who is God's person, one who knows God, who practices the presence of God, and hence is able to guide the community in doing likewise. In fact, the preacher's authority is not derived from the academy or from an ecclesiastical body but is inherent in his or her relation to God.

The other sense in which the author "relocates" the person in the pulpit is historical. Professor Northcutt does not return to the Augustine-Donatist debate over the relation of a minister's faith and character to the efficacy of that person's ministry. Rather, she recasts the minister's role as that of guide and director. In this new paradigm, the old debate is a nonissue.

This new paradigm is resourced by readings long and generally neglected by Protestant preachers: the Desert Fathers and Mothers, and mystics ancient and modern. Perhaps these saints have suffered benign neglect because many of us have bought the caricature: eccentric, lonely figures, in flight from the world, with clean washed hands and pensive faces, self-absorbed in exercises designed to avoid and to forget. What possibly could they say helpful to the pulpit? If you really want to know, read this book.

Without chastising us too much (a bit) for our neglect of the mystics, Northcutt lays out spiritual direction that is personal but not private, including not only the congregation but the world. Her preacher is socially sensitive, an intercessor and advocate for the oppressed, forgotten, and hurting, those struggling against systems that dehumanize, without neglecting the joy-filled and the strong. Her preacher as spiritual director does not allow experience to trump tradition but immerses herself/himself in tradition in order to experience it. Her preacher is thoughtful and studious, but not cerebral. If you approach this book with a fear of meeting excessive inwardness, you will jettison that fear early on.

Three features of the book are especially refreshing to me. One, the author has opened herself to listen to voices in the Roman Catholic tradition who have wisdom for the Protestant pulpit. Since Vatican II (1969) especially, the Roman Church has rediscovered the pulpit in refreshing and helpful ways. The rest of us need to pay attention. Two, Northcutt has learned that preaching can be sacramental without making it a sacrament. In this regard she is reminiscent of the insightful and suggestive work of Domenico Grasso. And three, the author restores God to the center of the sermon, its preparation, its delivery, and its reception. A generation ago, Professor Nils Dahl at Yale called our attention to the neglect of God in biblical and theological discourse. Obviously, Kay Northcutt was listening.

Professor Northcutt achieves this, and more, without the usual dance on the graves of those who have preceded her with books on preaching. In differentiating between her work and that of her predecessors, she clearly argues the place for her proposal without cartooning and harpooning. Respect for one's colleagues, living and dead, does not weaken the case for one's own work. On the contrary, even those who differ welcome the new volume. In fact, I am anxious to see what a church looks like whose preacher adopts this new paradigm.

Fred B. Craddock
Cherry Log, Georgia
October, 2008

PREFACE

THIS BOOK BEGAN AS A RESPONSE TO MY BELOVED students of preaching who, despite their brilliance and devotion to the art of preaching, exhibited consistent "gaps" in their sermons. God, for example, was rarely present in student sermons—apart from brief references—and spiritually formative sermon topics, such as vocation, spiritual formation, and spiritual direction of *congregations* were altogether missing. Perhaps most disheartening were the almost eight years of student sermons in which not a single reference was made to one of the great spiritual masters of the past twenty-one centuries of spiritual wisdom. That these gaps were consistent in kind and degree is all the more surprising considering that Phillips Theological Seminary gathers a student population representative of over twenty manifestations of Protestant denominations,[1] diverse in race and class, as well as gender and sexual orientation. The gaps that kept surfacing, in other words, were not a consequence of particular faiths, creeds, doctrines, or persons, but the result of a more universal and substantive lack of focus on "God" in particular and spirituality in general while preparing and delivering sermons.

What began as a simple noticing of "gaps" grew into my thesis (which grew into this book) for the Doctor of Ministry degree in Homiletics from Aquinas Institute of Theology in St. Louis, Missouri. I am grateful to my advisor for that thesis, the Reverend Doctor Gregory Heille, O.P., who is a consummate teacher. I consciously work daily to embody in my own teaching Greg's grace and generosity, wry patience, wisdom, steadfastness, encouragement, and sheer love of God. The all-too-popular litmus question, "What would Jesus do?" takes a variant form for me as associate professor of homiletics and worship at PTS. My question *always* is, "What would Greg do?"

Teresa of Avila noted that anyone who is trying to learn how to pray should spend as much time as possible with "friends of God." "Friend of God" beautifully describes my spiritual director, the Reverend Jill Clupper, and God is fortunate indeed to have found such a friend as Jill. The spiritual direction aspects of this book are a direct result of Jill's teaching, her devotion to Ignatian studies, and her profound investment of patience and wisdom toward my becoming a director.

My dearest beloved, Dr. Joe Bessler, was committed to this book, as he was to my doctoral studies at Aquinas. Joe read every word I wrote for these past years, cheering me on when discouraged, providing precisely the right insight when I needed it, all the while insisting on theological integrity in every word I produced. A cherished conversation partner devoted to the spiritual joy of Francis of Assisi, Joe has a keen sense of when to *laugh*— and how to help others laugh, too. For the grace of helping me laugh throughout my doctoral work and the writing of the book, I am indebted and grateful.

The Reverend Doctor Joseph R. Jeter Jr. was the reader for my doctoral thesis at Aquinas. His critical engagement of my ideas *and* his constant mentoring of me as preacher and scholar are inestimable. Words of gratitude fall short, though I hope someday to be as gentle, cautious, and gracious with future doctoral students of homiletics as Joey was with me.

I am grateful to my dean, the Reverend Doctor Don Pittman, and to my other colleagues at PTS who, during my semester-long writing leave, carried much of my load of academic advising and committee work. In a small seminary with too few faculty members to share the burden of the many administrative tasks, being relieved of advising and committee responsibilities for a semester is no small gift! Nor would the book have been completed without the sharp editing pencil of the Reverend Doctor William Tabbernee, president of PTS. President Tabbernee's consistent interest in the book provided confidence when my own was waning. The importance of a seminary president's good cheer and numerous cups of *café au lait* cannot be underestimated in the completion of a book.

My students at PTS have been steadfast in their enthusiasm for the book, their question always being *not* "Is it finished?" but "Can I buy a copy yet?" Their prayers for me during the writing of this book were my constant solace and companion. Especially I want to mention my students who preached daily homilies for Morning Prayer during my writing-leave absence: Debi Powell-Maxwell, Sheri Curry, and Sue Williams.

Three semesters of my PTS Advanced Preaching Workshop students pored over drafts of the book. Their careful reading of the text and their important questions regarding the "gaps" in my own thinking—were incredibly helpful and instructive! Those students include: Christy Dew, Linda Ewen, Victoria Fishel, Marcia Hagee, Joyce Hogan, Gina Jackson, Samuel Lee, Barry Loving, Carl Ownbey, and Mark Whitley (2006): Jacalyn Carter, Karen Clewell, Rebecca Highfield, Georgann Peck, Scott Taylor, Ulysses Washington, and Sue Williams (2007); Teresa Chapman, Natalie Ervin, Scott Foster, Steven Haney, David Massey-Brown, John Morrison III, Maureen Olson, LeAnn Sapp, Kathy Weaver, and Susan Whitely (2008).

I am particularly grateful to my research assistants during the span of this book's writing, Scott Taylor and Kathy Weaver. They spent hours in the PTS library researching books for me—including ordering countless interlibrary loans when needed. Both of them checked and double-checked endnotes, negotiated extended library-loan dates from our gracious PTS library, brought me cups of tea, attended to the minutiae of the bibliography, and cheered me on. The PTS librarians, Sandy Shapoval and Claire Powers, were invaluable to this project, their generosity and hospitality toward this book being borne out on virtually every page!

The members of my family, too, were among my chief cheerleaders. Dad and my elder sister Nancy read every word of the drafts. Their interest brought a joy which only a family can bring. I dearly wish my mother, Thelma Northcutt, could still have been alive to share in the thrill of book writing. My younger sister Amy (and her family) endured hours of phone calls listening to details only a younger sister could tolerate hearing in such minutiae. With the completion of each chapter, Amy sent a prize! And Nancy —when I was in the final throes—sent several important care packages. She possesses better than anyone a perfect sense of timing and reward.

My church, the Community of Hope United Church of Christ, in Tulsa, Oklahoma, never failed to ask (every Sunday, week after week after week for years now) how I was progressing in my studies and in the writing of the book. Julie Summers brought a fuschia pink begonia when chapters 1 and 2 refused to segue into chapter 3. Others wrote cards, sent e-mails, prayed, invited me to lunch, dinner, retreat, and parties. Especially I am grateful to my preaching feedback team: Sue, Geraldine, Anne, Julie T., Kirk, Bob, Julie S., and Donnie. Any preacher would count herself blessed to have such listeners and guides as you.

My cherished friend and traveling companion, Doctor Kristine Culp, planned a two-week victory tour of Florence, Assisi, Sienna, and Rome for the celebration of the project's completion. With such a tangible reward awaiting me there was no choice but to enjoy the work as it flew by.

A Fortress Press advance enabled me to rent, for a summer, a small farmhouse on the western prairie of Oklahoma where I was kept company by a thriving colony of mice, countless armadillos, turtles, skunks, birds, cattle, and an infinity of wheat farms as I finished chapters 4 and 5. I thank Fortress for the luxury of solitude, silence, and a rolling prairie's beauty as I finished the book. My gratitude also to Ivy Palmer Skrade for designing such an apt cover, that illustrates beautifully the heart of the book's thesis.

I have, throughout my life, read prefaces that simply glowed with gratitude for the editor. I now understand such prefaces fully. My editor, David Lott (to whom I was introduced by my beloved colleague, the Reverend Doctor Gary Peluso-Verdend), believed in this book from its inception. His constant guidance, good humor, challenge, and insight (Wait! Did I mention *patience?*) brought this book to fruition. May every writer be so fortunate as to have David Lott edit her work!

I am grateful for the opportunity to present an earlier version of chapter 1 at Harvard Divinity School in March 2004, for a ministry colloquium, *Crossing by Faith: Sermons on the Journey from Youth to Adulthood*, honoring Harry Baker Adams's brilliant ministry and the book (by the same name), edited by David Bartlett, Claudia Highbaugh, and Stephen B. Murray. Early drafts of chapters 2 and 3 were presented at Brite Divinity School's 2005 Kirkpatrick Summer Institute, Ghost Ranch, Santa Fe, New Mexico.

My beloved benefactors underwrote the expense of my education at Aquinas Institute of Theology which itself provided this book's foundation. Though such generosity can never be repaid, it fires a passionate devotion to teaching and preaching in hopes of being worthy of such confidence and investment.

Special thanks are due also to the trustees of Phillips Theological Seminary, not only for supporting my research and writing, but also for appointing me to the Fred B. Craddock Chair in Preaching and Worship, and to the Reverend Doctor Fred Craddock himself, for graciously agreeing to write the foreword for this book.

INTRODUCTION

As a scholar of the church who is also a spiritual director, professor of homiletics, and ordained pastor, I am convinced, as was the medieval mystic Meister Eckhart, that the God "who is a *thinked* God must become in some way a *present* God."[1] It is at the intersections—between "the thinked and the present God," between what can be known and what can only be intuited,[2] between what can be learned by cognition and what can be learned exclusively by loving, between what can be achieved through scholarship and what can be glimpsed only through listening to (and working with) those who suffer—that I live and teach. This book's hermeneutic affirms human capacities for cognitive knowing while simultaneously acknowledging, as did Evelyn Underhill, that some experiences are "never clear to the logical levels of the mind,"[3] and known therefore "more richly by intuition than it can ever be by intellect."[4] These ways of knowing are "beyond reason though not against reason."[5]

At the intersection of what can be known and what is unknowable, between the realm of human thought and intuition, there is Spirit—*ruah* or *pneuma*. This Spirit is alive, active, and elusively engages human persons, congregations, and the world toward liberation from whatever restrains us or constrains us from giving ourselves completely and generously to God—and God's hunger for *shalom*.

However well acquainted we may be with Scripture, reason, and tradition, many of us are virtual neophytes in the ways of the Spirit and practically illiterate when it comes to the themes, texts, curricula, and practices of the over twenty centuries of spiritual wisdom and formation available to us regarding the Spirit. We, as Christians and as church, are quite literally in dire need of those who can guide us toward our rightful inheritance, recovering patterns of intimacy with God, retracing the ways to invite, engage, and experience the liberating labors of the Holy Spirit. Historically, within Western Christian tradition, such guides have been known as spiritual directors.

This book proposes that preachers become as spiritual directors to their congregations, that preaching itself be a formational, sacramental act of spiritual direction, and that sermons *do* for congregations what spiritual direction does for individuals.

This book is also written with an urgent sense of concern for pastors and congregations. If the church does not soon pay vigilant attention to the need for spiritual guidance among its congregations, congregations will all too quickly be "reduced to a religious institution which is caretaker for an interesting history and cultural inheritance."[6] The postmodern mainline church teeters on the precarious balance between ghost walking in its past history and living abundantly out of that history; between becoming a lifeless *repository*, columbarium-like, of the ashes of its cultural inheritance and *expositor* of its life-giving, life-changing inheritance.

Likewise, this book is concerned for pastors who seek agility and steadfastness in their preaching and in their pastoral leadership. This book proposes that the preacher's spiritual life is as foundational to preaching as brilliant scriptural exegesis and breathtaking sermon delivery. Further, it explores the formation and nurture of preachers' interior lives, proposing methods and models toward enlivening the preacher's interior life within the peculiar and highly specific demands visited upon us by this postmodern era.

My model of preaching as spiritual direction is driven by two interdependent interests: (1) congregational renewal, and (2) the renewal of the spiritual and preaching life of pastors. The hermeneutic of preaching as spiritual direction is for pastors who desire a model of preaching that can renew and deepen both their inner spirit and their sense of vocation. Additionally, during this era when pastors seem to hold virtually no *positional* authority in congregational life, teetering toward becoming mere placeholders (or committee-ward dispute managers), preaching as spiritual direction is a model (and a metaphor) that provides a real sense of religious authority, of how pastors are, quite simply, to *be* the "God-person" and guide of their congregation (see chapter 3).

This method's interest for renewal of congregations is based upon their becoming a *paideuterion*—a school for wisdom—bringing into focus the questions with which congregations are struggling. It reformulates congregational ethos. In a time and place that is increasingly suspicious of strangers and of those who are different from us, preaching as spiritual direction is a hermeneutic that suggests how we build community, a view of church that emboldens the kin-dom, kindling the courage and wisdom to—with God's help—work toward God's kin-dom come on earth.

Spiritual Direction

Spiritual direction cultivates attentiveness, specifically the ability to *notice* God's presence and activity in one's life and in the world. Spiritual direction, typically, is a one-to-one relationship between a spiritual director and a directee, comprised of a meeting between directee and director once a month (for approximately an hour in length). Begun and ended with spoken prayer, these sessions include lengthy periods of listening and silence. A commitment to spiritual direction reflects a conscientious commitment to tend one's relationship with God, to listen deeply to one's life, to explore gently the uncharted terrain of one's spiritual landscape, and tenderly cultivate one's vocation. Margaret Guenther, writer and spiritual director, describes spiritual direction as "holy listening," both for what might constrain us from responding more fully to God as well as for those events, images, relationships, and sufferings that illuminate more brightly the God to whom one's life is authentically drawn.[7]

Spiritual direction is a way to practice accountability for one's spiritual development. More clinically put, spiritual direction is "an interpersonal situation in which one person assists another to develop and come to greater maturity in the life of the spirit that is faith, hope, and love."[8] Even though spiritual direction is built on a relationship, it is not like the exchange that happens among friends, nor is it instructional, nor primarily problem solving, nor answer giving, nor advice dispensing, though it is rooted in the dynamic of listening. A spiritual director is not a therapist, a counselor, or an analyst but a trained, "mature, skilled Christian to whom we choose to be accountable for our spiritual life."[9]

Additionally, spiritual direction awakens the directee to what spiritual director Carolyn Gratton has called "the full range of the human heart, mind, soul, and strength."[10] This noticing (and awakening) through "holy listening" orients us to God, to living more purposefully and more fully into our vocation, and to the intentional shaping of our lives into a more generous response to God.

Though many posit Jesus as the "first" spiritual director and therefore note the art and care of spiritual direction as having begun with him, spiritual direction was more specifically and expressly pioneered in the deserts of Egypt in the third through the fifth centuries. What developed from the first monastic flowerings in the desert has become a rich, diverse tradition of Christian teaching, a re-creation or representation of that history will be not be attempted here except to say that what soon became a Catholic and predominantly male tradition typically practiced in the West by Caucasian persons can no longer, in the twenty-first century, be qualified by or limited to such aspects. Spiritual direction today is practiced by Protestants and Catholics and Orthodox of every color, race, ethnicity, and class.

Communally and congregationally speaking, spiritual direction seeks to implement God's longing for *shalom*, God's hope for wholeness in human persons and communities. Spiritual direction guides not only persons as individuals but congregations as a whole into moment-by-moment tending of the holy. Though spiritual direction produces nothing tangible, its progress is measured by a growth in compassion: for self, others, earth, and world. It wakes congregations up, reminding us that congregational life is not "scripted," but a complex, collaborative process in which we "write" our lives as individuals, families, and congregations in light of God's presence.

Finally, spiritual direction is a process for discerning our vocation, for discovering, as Walter Brueggemann puts it, how our "purpose for being in the world . . . is related to the purposes of God."[11] Preaching as spiritual direction searches for and speaks to a congregation's vocation as certainly as spiritual direction guides an individual in discerning vocation.

Put theologically, spiritual direction assumes the operation of God, or grace, already present in the felt promptings and desire of the seeker to experience and understand the call and presence of God in her or his life. By way of analogy, spiritual direction presumes what James Carroll writes about prayer: "I presume that, since the Spirit lives in me already, I am already prone to pray."[12]

Theological Assumptions

While my hermeneutic of preaching as spiritual direction is broad enough to embrace theologies as diverse as those of evangelicals, liberalists, feminists, liberationists, and postliberals, it seems nonetheless somewhat disingenuous not to declare what *I* mean when I utilize the word *God*, particularly within the pages of a book dedicated to a hermeneutic of preaching whose conscious intent and explicit purpose is "all about God."

Somewhat like Canadian theologian Douglas John Hall, my theology draws upon both postliberal and revisionist schools of thought.[13] With the postliberal school I am rethinking Christian faith from resources within the tradition. I aim to restore and reassert the wisdom of ancient spiritual patterns and disciplines from tradition and the church, as Sirach 44:15 puts it, "Let the peoples declare the wisdom of the saints!" I presume that the moral and spiritual concerns of moderns and postmoderns are uncannily like those of our forebears in the faith, and that classical Christian texts (Bible, patristic, medieval texts—particularly the Desert Fathers, Mothers, and mystics) remain pivotal resources for our spiritual life, individually and collectively. Yet I also draw upon the liberal theologies of my divinity school studies at the University of Chicago, particularly David Tracy's revisionist model of theology in which retrieval of traditions and texts must be reinterpreted or "reappropriated" in light of contemporary experience.[14]

Gordon Kaufman's notion of God as a symbol of orientation that can "help draw us, or drive us, beyond our present ideals and values into a new and open future transcending anything we today can even imagine"[15] helps me understand how God enables humanity to participate in a new and alternative reality. When I use the word *prayer*, for example, I understand it to be first and foremost a verb, an alternative form of discourse, an activity through which God—who calls us to an alternative reality—is construed. Prayer (like the work of poetry and fine art) imagines or construes the alternative reality in which God dwells; prayer *speaks* it into being. Prayer relies upon imagination, where, of course, the Holy Spirit lives, and breathes, and enjoys. Prayer resists a "dynamic of exchange" in favor of purposive language that transforms, confesses, communes, and hopes all things. God as alternative reality is what I understand myself to be praying into being when I pray. It is my attempt to step into the inside of an alternative universe where God begins to be, so that our human imagination (beginning with *mine*) catches a glimpse of that alternative possibility. In that glimpse we are changed, as is the current, conventional "reality." An aperture opens up, as Walter Wink puts it, a place where God can *be*.[16]

We easily miss glimpses of this God as "alternative reality," because, typically, it is difficult to apprehend and pay attention to what is utterly unfamiliar and completely unexpected. But this is what Jesus presents to us in his parables and in the parabolic activity of miracles. Consequently, parables and miracles are among the best places to locate the God of alternative reality about which I speak, write, and pray. The miracle of nonviolence as exemplified in the peaceful end of apartheid in South Africa, when Bishop Desmond Tutu, Nelson Mandela, and so many others continually held out an alternative reality of nonviolence and peace—not revenge—as the end of apartheid. The miracle of nonviolence that peacefully integrated the lunch counters of Nashville's Woolworth's store in the United States. The miracle of nonviolence called Solidarity that broke the oppressive dominance of communism in a shipyard in Gdansk, Poland.

This God *is* cosmic creativity holding open not only the future but the past, and human persons, for their part, are creative, historical beings, open to receiving the incarnate impulses at work in all creation. The human capacity for being *moved*—by beauty, by moral virtue, by suffering—underscores my anthropology of attraction and attention, itself reliant upon habits of spiritual practices, wakefulness, resilience, and acuity. Jesus consistently taught an anthropology of attention; from oil in our lamps to considering the lilies we are to dwell in a constant state of readiness, wakefulness, and awareness.[17] With Elizabeth Johnson and other feminists I understand God as *Sophia*-wisdom most especially incarnate in Jesus' life and ministry within first-century Palestine.[18] Christ is less a specific content of doctrine or belief, than a flexible, living activity among us, breaking open whatever limits or constricts us from opening to God.

Hermeneutical Assumptions

While paying rigorous attention to exegesis and the finest historical-critical work available, pastors who bring a hermeneutic of spiritual direction to bear upon their preaching will find within scriptural texts a rich array of images, characters, conflicts, and themes fruitful for the formation and guidance of both persons and congregations. Viewed from the lens of spiritual direction, the sermon becomes an occasion that not only orients us to God and to biblical stories of God's activity, *but also to the curriculum, methods, and practices of being formed as a people of God.* Though all preaching is scripturally based, preaching as spiritual direction will specifically utilize the major themes of spiritual direction (discussed in chapter 4) as hermeneutical lenses. These hermeneutical lenses function as discovery points of encounter with the biblical message.

With Tracy, who has suggested that biblical criticism and its exploration of various structural interconnections of the text within its original setting may aid—but cannot be fully adequate to—the full hermeneutical encounter between text and interpreter,[19] I believe the texts and traditions of spiritual direction help us risk a deeper engagement with the biblical texts. For the pastor, preaching as spiritual direction, its life-giving themes (chapter 4), and balancing pairs (chapter 5), facilitate that deeper hermeneutical encounter for which Tracy calls.

Further, affirming that God is present in and through the world, preaching as spiritual direction celebrates biblical poetry and narratives as vital to the religious community's identity but also explores contemporary experience for signs of God's presence and guidance. Preaching as spiritual direction wakes us up and alerts us to the presence of God stirring in our midst. More than awakening our consciousness in a general sense, preaching as spiritual direction moves us to behold that presence in our ordinary, moment-to-moment experience so that we might be responsive to and responsible for nurturing our continued attentiveness, and response, to God's needs in the world as well as to our own—and to that of our suffering neighbors. Insofar as such preaching encourages habits of attentive beholding and responding, it also guides the vocational development of both persons and the congregation as a whole, providing the basis for the narrative of the congregation's distinctive religious journey and identity.[20]

Chapter 1 explores formation by attraction as an apt model of preaching as spiritual formation for persons and congregations, particularly in this era known as postmodernity. Chapter 2 places preaching as spiritual direction in historical context by taking a look at recent homiletic history, specifically by analyzing the profoundly influential late-modern model of preaching as counseling for both it strengths and liabilities. Chapter 3 searches the wisdom of the Desert Fathers and Mothers, mystics, and reformers looking to them for guidance—both as role models and also in matters of content for preaching as spiritual direction. Chapter 4 explores six classic themes from the history of spiritual direction to inform preaching as spiritual direction. Chapter 5 retrieves and reappropriates several classic balancing "operative pairs" in spiritual direction for today's preacher. Finally, the book concludes with several sample sermons that demonstrate preaching as spiritual direction, along with a schema that directs the actual process of writing a sermon which seeks to preach as spiritual direction and guidance on the practice of *lectio divina*.

1 | FORMATION
BY ATTRACTION

CHICAGO, 1986

Theologian Joseph Sittler was fully reclined in his easy chair, eyes closed, deeply relaxed. Blind from complications of old age, Sittler relied upon a small cadre of volunteer readers (mainly graduate students) who took shifts each day, reading to Sittler the books he dearly missed poring over with his own eyes. One afternoon Sittler asked me to read a handful of Emily Dickinson poems to him. In the long silence that followed I could hear Sittler memorizing Dickinson's words, inscribing them on his heart. Though beginning to die of old, good age—even then Sittler was busy imprinting images in his mind's eye.

It so happened that on this particular day I was armed with an agenda beyond that of afternoon-shift reader. Enrolled in (and enthralled by) my first homiletics course at the University of Chicago Divinity School, I interrupted Sittler's holy silence, inquiring, "What does it mean—effective preaching? What does it mean for the disoriented, postmodern, sort-of-lost, sidelined American church we love? What does it look like? How does it work?"

Sittler sat bolt upright so abruptly that his recliner snapped to attention. Although he was blind, he locked eyes with me and practically shouted, "You preachers must be vehement as hell about the perfectly obvious! Remember when Jesus came to Lazarus, and *wept*? How the crowd remarked, amazed, 'See how he loved him!'? Take that amazement—that passionate love of

God—into the pulpit. *That's* how effective preaching works. The church—*your* church—will be astonished.

"Preachers must *reveal* their passionate love of God in the pulpit. Their church members will go home Sunday afternoon, just like those onlookers who were amazed by Jesus' tears, wondering, 'Where do *I* get that kind of aliveness—*that* kind of love?'" Sittler paused for a long while then mused, "Human spirituality—which is latent within each of us—must be *evoked*. You preachers must awaken the human spirit like a fire alarm. Great preaching evokes cognition by amazement."

Sittler's words stayed with me as I made my way from graduate school through ordination and into my first pastorate in Fort Worth, Texas. I gathered up my love of God and carried it into the pulpit with me each Sunday. But after three years of congregational ministry—organizing educational programs, supervising youth pastors, daily visits to congregants in local hospitals, preaching, attending ecumenical councils and social justice meetings, reporting at board meetings about endless other congregational committees—I was burnt out. I was spent. Empty. Only then did it dawn on me that Sittler's advice (preachers must "*reveal*" their passionate love of God") surfaces *two* interdependent and inseparable issues: preaching *and* the preacher's spiritual life.

Prior to entering congregational ministry I had naïvely presumed that the various tasks of ministry would themselves deepen and develop my love of God. But over the course of those first three years of parish ministry my rhetorical skills as a preacher dramatically increased while, ironically, the demands of ministry wore away at my love of God (like an undertow). Three years into the pastorate I was exhausted not only physically and emotionally, but also spiritually. I'd been extremely busy working *for* God—in hopes that my vocation itself would draw me closer to God—but paradoxically my vocation depleted that most intimate of relationships, the relationship between God and self.

I needed God and I needed to pray. But I did not know how.

LEBH SHOMEA, TEXAS, 1989

Seriously burnt out and disoriented, I made my first seven-day silent retreat to Lebh Shomea's House of Prayer, located on twenty thousand acres of desert (near Sarita, Texas). Lebh Shomea has two hermits and a priest in residence. I made a reservation for seven days and nights.

I packed my laptop, which carried the manuscript for a book of prayers I hoped to finish. It took two days to get there, first by plane, then by a taxi to the bus station, followed by a long bus ride to a "flag-stop." There, my bag and I were dropped ignobly on the side of the highway, with nary a town, building, or person in sight. Finally, a tie-dye-patterned pickup truck (apparently put together by spare parts of former monastery pickups) pulled off on the highway—to retrieve me.

I was escorted to a tiny hermitage, left there all alone, surrounded by palm trees, javelinas, flocks of wild turkey, white-tailed deer, scrub oaks, rattlesnakes, and silence. Big as a sonic boom, the silence pressed in on me with centrifugal force. Lebh Shomea offers not only silence, but a library with an astounding collection of the classics of Western and Eastern spirituality—as well as spiritual direction—for anyone who makes a retreat there. I signed up for (what was to me a completely unfamiliar thing) "spiritual direction," figuring "it can't hurt and it just *might* help."

Three days later a teensy scrap of paper pinned to the "Communication Board" informed me that my direction session would commence at 10:30 *that* morning. Not having spoken (or been spoken to) for seventy-two hours and jittery about what on earth I'd gotten myself into, I nervously sat with Sister Marie in silence, the palms of my hands slightly damp. Marie is one of the two hermits I mentioned earlier. She carries silence with her as palpably as most of us carry our overscheduled lives. I tried to make it—the power of Marie's silence—stop. I chatted about my book manuscript, about my church, about how worn out I was until finally I succumbed to Marie's silence.

After what seemed to have been an hour of holding silence together, I startled like a frightened rabbit when Marie quietly asked, "Why has God called you to this desert?" Shocked, I found the silence had wrung the truth out of me: "I'm in this desert because I feel God-forsaken." Marie then directed me to consider how I intended to spend the next four days in "the desert" to which God had called me. I regressed backwards into Chatty-Cathy mode, going on and on about having brought my laptop to finish the draft of my book—and that I'd already checked out a couple of armloads of books from Lebh Shomea's library—blah, blah, blah.

Marie sat, visibly stunned, silent. Minutes passed with only my rapid heartbeat interrupting the silence. Then my newfound director asked incredulously, "God has called you to this desert—and now you're going to *avoid* God?!" Her eyes, brown and liquid and seemingly omniscient, met mine. She then "directed," "No computer. No work. No books. You only have four days. God has called you here. Be obedient and *listen*."

She then guided me to think back, When as a child was I most aware of God's presence, care, and love? Immediately the nine-year-old little girl I had been leapt into view. I said as much. Marie then directed me toward reengaging that nine-year-old girl: how she felt, thought, moved, played, and had her being in God; to stay outdoors "beholding" the beauty and goodness of God's creation as I retrieved the memory of being deeply beloved by God. And she added emphatically, "No reading *or* laptop work until the moon rises each night."

I spent the days bicycling, hiking, watering thirsty plants, and watching the day unfold hour by hour, as I had when nine years old. Lebh Shomea is inhabited by small, white-tailed deer—and is, by the way, beastly hot even in May when I retreated there. The cultivated grounds are nourished by huge sprinkler systems. In the late afternoons, fawns play in the sprinklers as do countless rainbows. I knew my recovery of the nine-year-old was progressing when several days after my meeting with Sister Marie I silently strolled through the sprinklers with the fawns. I hadn't been that quiet or content in years.

But upon moonrise on the *first* night following Sister Marie's direction, I was relieved to return to reading. I began to make the acquaintance of Teresa of Avila through her autobiography.[1] Teresa's candor, her quickness to laugh, and her fully-aliveness brought to mind the nine-year-old girl that I had been—but in the fully grown-up form of a very wise, formidable, compassionate woman. I had at last found a teacher who could take me by the hand and guide me in how to love and be loved by God, how to delight in God, and be hospitable toward God. I watched her, listened to her, even found myself sharing her frustrations, but most of all I absorbed her wisdom on *how to pray*. With Teresa guiding me I learned how to take God as friend. Her voice and insight taught me how to pay attention to God and how to cultivate daily an interior life capable of withstanding the demands of pastoral leadership.

Lebh Shomea's penetrating silence and the guidance of my spiritual director—along with wisdom from that amazing luminary of spiritual development, Teresa of Avila—resuscitated me. But they also exposed the assumption upon which Sittler's insight into preaching rests: fully alive preaching (that awakens the human spirit "like a fire alarm") relies upon a preacher's fully-aliveness in God. Fully-aliveness does *not* mean such preachers are immune to "dry" periods in their spiritual lives nor that are they protected from the dark night of the soul. Fully-aliveness *does* mean that "always and in all ways" these preachers are seeking God and guidance of spiritual wisdom. Even in the dark night. Even in the desert. Even in the rough patch. God.

I discovered at Lebh Shomea that paying attention to God is like every other human competency (whether baking a cake, reading a book, or learning how to feel empathy): it must be learned. Just like learning to ride a bike—first with training wheels and eventually with a loving adult running alongside providing balance—we also learn how to be with God. That is precisely how spiritual direction functions. Spiritual directors guide human persons in learning God: how to love and be loved by God, how to delight in God, and how to be hospitable toward God, how to suffer with God. Spiritual direction runs alongside preachers, providing ballast and balance.

This book proposes that a preacher's receptivity to God and the lifelong process of spiritual formation are foundational to preaching. Preachers themselves, it follows, need guidance (like that offered by a spiritual director), wisdom from great spiritual teachers (like Teresa of Avila), and patterns of spiritual practices that restore balance (like silent retreat, prayerful reading, and delighting in nature). So do congregations! Consequently, this book also proposes that preaching's aim is not only awakening individual human spirits but also those of congregations. Perhaps most radically, this book proposes that a sermon's purpose is spiritual direction. Preaching as spiritual direction orients congregations toward increasing their attentiveness to God, their compassion for one another, and their vocational clarity, particularly in regard to the congregation's work toward God's *shalom*. The increase of each of these three components is essential. They work together interdependently for the purpose of "seeking God always in all ways."

In this opening chapter I suggest that modern, twentieth-century theories of Christian preaching have emphasized hermeneutical and rhetorical techniques, prioritizing the *how* of preaching over the *aim* of preaching. While both helpful and necessary, such theories have presumed—or avoided—any serious discussion of (1) the love of God, (2) the preacher's spiritual formation, and (3) the spiritual formation of congregations. I then turn to a key component of spiritual direction: receptivity, tracing its logic from childhood to adulthood. Next, I develop "formation by attraction" (itself a component of receptivity) through which humans learn God. An exploration of sacramental aspects of preaching as spiritual direction *and* an example of a formational pastor, George Herbert, follow.

Finally, I propose a paradigm shift regarding the *aim* of preaching, from the previous generations' emphases upon *persuasion, explanation, communication,* to that of *formation*.[2] Preaching as spiritual direction (by pastors who intentionally view themselves as spiritual guides) cultivates habits of attentiveness and receptivity within the preacher on the one hand while inculcating an ethos of spiritual formation and vocational purpose within congregations on the other.

The Modern Homiletic Landscape

Sittler's exhortation that preachers "awaken the human spirit like a fire alarm" presumes not only that God has tenderly breathed into each person (and congregation) the genesis of spirituality but also that preaching can enliven it. French existentialist and Christian philosopher Gabriel Marcel inadvertently yet vividly captured an aspect of what Sittler intended by "enlivening," as witnessed by Father Murray Bodo, O.F.M.,[3] who observed Marcel giving a lecture on the "Theatre of the Absurd." Immediately following Marcel's lecture one of the participants asked Marcel,

"How did you come to know God?" Marcel answered simply, "I came to know God by loving someone in whom God dwelt." Marcel was *attracted* to God by someone in whom God dwelt. Marcel's experience is not unique. Human persons—in whom God's love is transparent—attract others to God.

Inquire of virtually any Christian, lay or ordained, "How did you come to know God?" and inevitably the answer—both immediate and heartfelt—is the *name* of a person in whom "God dwelt," whether it be a beloved pastor, Sunday school teacher, church camp counselor, aunt, grandfather, or caring neighbor. We are attracted to God through God's transparent activity revealed in human persons. Yet an emphasis on the preacher's love of God is *not* where most homiletic books begin! While theories and models of preaching presume a devotion to the "good news" of God's saving work through Christ, rarely do theories or models of preaching focus on the preacher's receptivity and responsiveness to God. Nor do homileticians typically acknowledge the central purpose of preaching as that of the *spiritual formation* of Christians and congregations. Little explicit attention is given to *preaching* as spiritual formation or to the spiritual formation of the preacher. The cultivation of the congregation's love of God (and interior landscape—what Gerard Manley Hopkins called the "inscape"), homiletically speaking, is presumed or, worse, left to chance.

There are several understandable reasons *why* recent homiletic theory has not explicitly emphasized the pastor's love of God nor prioritized the sermon *as* spiritual direction. Historically speaking, preaching for the past century has been preoccupied by other matters! During the Second Great Awakening up through the nineteenth century the purpose of North American preaching was that of persuading individuals to an "act of decision" to become a Christian.[4] Preaching's principal project was that of saving souls.

In the middle of the nineteenth century homiletic theory shifted the aim of preaching from *persuasion* to *explanation*.[5] In the early twentieth century a new word emerged in homiletic textbooks: the illustration, and as Tom Long put it, "the preacher as persuader was being replaced by the preacher as explainer."[6] The modern sermon was informational and propositional, seeking to reconcile Christian tradition with a scientific worldview.

The purpose of such preaching was "the clear, logical, and rational presentation of ideas derived from the gospel."[7] Preaching as explanation was a homiletic response to the unique anxiety "modern" science posed for Christianity. Explanatory sermons negotiated the intellectual power of science and technology, reconciling them with biblical theology and Christian tradition. Homileticians emphasized the "how" of preaching with attention to sermonic structure, the use of analogical disciplines such as modern psychology to "diagnose" and "help" the problems of the modern soul, and rhetorical devices to hold the congregation's interest. In many ways the perfecter of this explanatory form of preaching was the brilliant Harry Emerson Fosdick, who simultaneously grafted his distinctive variation onto it: "preaching as counseling." Fosdick's profound influence upon preaching remains today.[8]

In response to unique issues surfacing in the 1960s, including the displacement of authority, the predominance of visual and mass media, and the advent of new theories of rhetoric and criticism, Fred Craddock brought forth his brilliant inductive method of preaching. He and others belonging to the New Homiletic[9] sought the end of the discursive three-point-thesis sermon inherited from explanatory sermons of earlier "modernity," shifting preaching's emphasis from *persuasion* and *explanation* to *communication*. The initiators of the New Homiletic noticed not only that the local church pastor's authority was eroding but also that the congregation's attention span was sharply diminishing—and conjectured it just might have something to do with *how* preachers were approaching the art and design of the sermon. Predictably, the New Homiletic emphasized the *how* of preaching: Craddock's inductive sermon, Eugene Lowry's loop, David Buttrick's moves. Later developments include Long's Witness-Bearer[10] and Ron Allen's teaching sermon[11] model, to name but a few. Thomas Troeger also contributed to the strength of the inductive sermon through proposing a sermon's rhetoric be *visual*—playing like a DVD or videotape—in the mind's eye of the congregation.[12]

At a very basic level, modern homiletics took for granted the process of formation (both congregational and pastoral) as something that "happened" in church, in sermons, and in Sunday school. The New Homiletic rarely mentions classical practices of spiritual formation or the spiritual life of the preacher. Neither is there an emphasis on such topics as a preacher's intimacy with God or preaching as spiritual direction of congregations. The New Homiletician emphasized *how* to preach by developing fast-paced plot turns, unpredictable reversals on scriptural texts, and purposefully inconclusive conclusions. The driving force of the New Homileticians was *method* for the purpose of sermons being *heard*.

This book emphasizes the "what" of preaching. Rather than enfolding the aim of preaching within a proposed *method* this book reverses that order. It seeks to enfold method within the *aim* of preaching, bringing into balance the previous generation's astounding contribution to *how* to preach with a conscientious return to guiding preaching toward the *what* of preaching. The paradigm of preaching as spiritual direction *guides* what is prefocal, not conscious in human persons—and what is sensed or perceived by congregations—into what is known, focal, conscious.[13] Such preaching is spiritual formation, awakening hearts (and congregations) to receive life as a mystery to be lived, rather than a problem to be solved.

This book proposes that preaching's aim be that of spiritual formation for congregations and the individuals that comprise them. Regardless of theological and denominational context and in the midst of a hugely diverse span of class, race, gender, sexual orientation, age, and ecclesiology, preaching's purpose is that of spiritual formation of individuals and their communities of faith. While I will provide some suggestions regarding the "how" of preaching as spiritual direction, my focus and central concern will be the *aim* of preaching, the process of forming congregations toward the love and desire of God.

The Pastor's Formation

A second reason why homiletic theory has not (in the recent past century) explicitly prioritized the pastor's love of God or the sermon's aim as spiritual direction lies within the broader context of pastoral formation. The completion of a Master of Divinity degree (the current professional standard of pastoral formation) requires demonstrating competencies in theology, church history, ethics,

Bible, church polity, and doctrine—and in the arts and practices of ministry such as preaching, worship, and pastoral care.

While seminaries and divinity schools have been successful in the academic and practical formation of pastors, the same cannot always be said regarding the *spiritual* formation of pastors in general and preachers in particular. As homiletician Richard Lischer muses, "Despite the wave of spirituality in both the church and popular culture today . . . Protestant homiletics has avoided the larger issues of the spiritual formation of preachers."[14] Eugene Peterson further illumines this problem, noting, "People are fed up with leaders who talk learnedly and officiously about God but . . . don't seem connected to a relationship with God."[15] In many seminaries and divinity schools *formation* remains largely elusive, it being taken for granted that spiritual formation occurs "naturally," something that is "caught" rather than "taught." Peterson's insight belies the unhappy divide between the academic discipline's emphasis upon *thinking about* God and the pastoral leader's responsibility of *being with* God.

Yet thinking about God differs from being with God, just as thinking about becoming a parent differs from nuzzling a newborn infant at the breast or disciplining a teenager who misses curfew. Even something as "natural" as nursing or disciplining a child—something we had imagined would simply happen instinctually—is in fact complicated and must necessarily be *learned* by both infant and parent. In the same way, what we (and our seminaries and divinity schools) hoped or imagined would be instinctive and "natural" (namely our love of and creaturely dependence upon God) is not. A "natural" unfolding of spiritual development cannot be assumed in seminarians or in congregations. Surprisingly (and counterintuitively), one's relationship with God, the practice of receptivity for God, must be *learned*. Creating a curriculum and guidance for learning such attentiveness to God is the explicit purpose of spiritual direction.

Pastors who are best capable of guiding congregations in developing attentiveness to and receptivity for God (as well as God's needs in the world) are those who have themselves been *guided* in the art and process of cultivating receptivity to God. The presumption that all pastors are indeed familiar with or intimate with God (and that preaching emerges from this bond between pastor and God) is illustrated by Sister Pascaline (Superior of the Benedictine sisters in Sand Springs, Oklahoma, where I often retreat). Sister Pascaline recently asked me, "What are you writing?" When I responded, "I'm writing a little book proposing God be the subject of most every sermon and that the purpose of preaching is spiritual formation," Sister Paschaline's eyes widened with disbelief. She blinked hard several times as if stunned by my proposal—then exclaimed, "How can preaching be anything *but* spiritual direction and all about God?" Yet, as John McClure and others point out, God does not play a central role in mainstream Protestant sermons.[16] The relative displacement of God (and absence of spiritual formation) in preaching has become patently clear to me after a decade of teaching homiletics. Student sermons that deal explicitly with formational topics such as vocation, contemplation, cultivation of the interior life, listening for God, and developing the art of attention in prayer are few and far between. When God *does* appear in student sermons, typically God is a mere referent or sign. God as subject is surprisingly— and soberingly—rare. Even within the (numerically) dominant sermons on doctrinal and pastoral concerns God makes rare appearances, serving only as referent, virtually never as *subject.*

Preachers who are reticent to reveal their love of God in an existential, personal way deprive their listeners of a vital aspect of formation: modeling intimacy with God from one's being receptive, responsive toward God.[17] Homiletics as well as nature abhors a vacuum and the mainline church's failure to speak personally and forcefully about God has left both the public and the church wide open for an "American spirituality that is all about us: fulfilling our potential, getting the blessings of God, expanding our influence, finding our gifts. . . ."[18] Such an "American spirituality" is purpose driven in an acquisitive, consuming way that reflects North American culture, with a virtually willful rejection of noticing (paying attention to) the suffering neighbor.

By contrast, spiritual direction intentionally practices the fine art of *shaping* attentiveness both to God *and* to God's needs in this world: to *see* our neighbors' suffering and to respond. Such attentiveness must be cultivated—not only in seminarians and pastors, but also in congregations and the individuals who comprise them. Spiritual direction is a wisdom tradition that has been conscientiously developed over a span of twenty centuries for the express purpose of enriching the human person's attentiveness to God. It's an apt guide for preaching in this disoriented, hungry-for-God, postmodern era.

Receptivity from Childhood through Adulthood

Roman Catholic theologian Karl Rahner noted that human beings are highly susceptible to catching a sense of purposeful-ness in—and with—God during childhood.[19] The awakening of a vocational call, often originating in childhood, typically unfolds gradually until, chrysalis-like, it emerges in adulthood. This early receptivity during childhood to the *attracting* God, such as I experienced as a nine-year-old, is exhibited in the uninhibited and engaging spaces of imagination and play—as well as the remarkably heightened sensitivity children experience in every taste, smell, sight, touch, and sound. No detail is too small, no issue too large to explore: "Dad, why *is* the sky blue?"; "Mom, where was I . . . *before* I was born?"

The dramatic openness to God as experienced in childhood in the seemingly inexhaustible amount of time available contrasts sharply with the constricting schedule of the pastorate—where the incessant demand for the pastor's attention effectively eviscer-ates time for solitude and play; for the reading, reflecting, and restorative leisure necessary to nourish the preacher's most pri-mary relationship: intimacy with God. Paradoxically, pastors who were initially *drawn* to ministry through God's activity in their lives find themselves caught in the throes of a vocation that is *driven* by the time-consuming demands of the church. Quiet, intimate, regenerative time for drawing into God is gradually suffocated by congregational activities. A vocation begun as a response to the attracting God—and with the hope of awakening "the human spirit like a fire alarm"—gives way to an endless stream of unpredictable congregational crises coming at the pastor "like telephone poles seen from a speeding train." Not surprisingly, God, and time *for* God, is displaced from the center. The pastor's initial, nascent sense of call is muted by incoming calls, newsletter deadlines, and irascible congregants. Time and space necessary to practice receptivity to God are eliminated. Slowly but surely, one day at a time, the work of ministry eliminates the sheer silence in which the attracting God insists on speaking (1 Kgs. 19:11-12).

Even pastors' physical bodies become endangered when God is displaced. The constant pastoral demands—combined with delayed rest and prayer and rejuvenation—can escalate into unbearably high levels of frustration, too often sanitized with self-medication (be it alcohol, drugs, or hyper-commitment), all of which conspire to produce carelessness for physical (along with spiritual) well-being. Tragically, clergy are "the top" among occupations "dying of heart disease."[20] One might argue it's a hazard of the profession—everyone wants to take their pastor to breakfast, lunch, or dinner. But pastors' sedentary lifestyles, combined with attempts to meet near impossible demands, take an immense toll on their well-being. Preachers' bodies can themselves become inhospitable to God.

One of the greatest strengths of Protestant formation of both persons and congregations is the highly activistic pursuit of God through doing, worshiping, potlucking, and attending committee meetings. We are quite skilled at shaping ourselves into Christians and congregations through communal activities. Even church "clean-up days" for weeding the flowerbeds and pruning the bushes become a good excuse for eating lunch together, sharing life, laughter, and one another's gifts and burdens. But too much *activity* without its balance and best friend, receptivity, actually impedes God's work within us and our congregations. The concept of receptivity *for* God is a largely unexplored region of the American Protestant church and the people who inhabit its pews, though it runs like a plumb line through classical spiritual texts including the Bible. The Sabbath command is a clarion call that human persons protect one day each week for rest, pleasure, and enjoyment for the purpose of paying attention to God and the goodness of creation.

Years ago, when, as described above, I first sought the monastic desert retreat of Lebh Shomea for a week of silence, renewal, and spiritual direction, I carried an extra suitcase filled with a small truckload of church work to "finish." My spiritual director forbade me to do *any* work and advised, "Stay outside all day. *Listen for the God who called you to this silence.*" I was shocked by the difficulty of doing so. At the end of the first day spent entirely outdoors at Lebh Shomea (walking, bicycling, resting, watering the retreat house's thirsty plants, and hiking) I glimpsed that it was not only my *interior* self that had become terribly out of shape. I was a wreck *physically*, too. As I began to reacquaint myself with the God I had left behind decades ago in my childhood, I couldn't help but notice that part of practicing receptivity to God (as prescribed by my spiritual director) required lots of fresh air and physical exertion—along with wandering, silence, solitude, leisure, sitting and looking at nothing and everything. Just like when I was a child![21]

Pastors especially must face the daily dilemma of *how* to practice receptivity in the midst of a daunting schedule of *activity* for God. How can pastors practice attentiveness in the midst of distraction? Mystic and reformer Teresa of Avila put it this way:

> The soul collects wood and does all it can by itself, but finds no way of kindling the fire of the love of God. [The soul is] . . . driving itself crazy with blowing on the fire and rearranging the wood, yet all its efforts only put out the fire more and more. We should remember . . . how great is the love God has revealed to us . . . [and] ever strive to awaken our own love of God. . . . Then the Lord comes back and *kindles* it . . .[22]

Clearly the imbalance between activity *for* God and simply *being with* (waiting for) God is not a new problem. Teresa of Avila—who single-handedly founded, built, and raised the monies to support seventeen Discalced Carmelite convents, and is one among only three women granted the title "Doctor of the Church"[23]—herself struggled to achieve a healthy give-and-take between activity and receptivity. Even this most famous, amazing, and incomprehensibly effective nun had to remind herself—and the Carmelite sisters under her care—to alternate between activity and quietly "being" so that God can "kindle the fire." Today's preachers and pastors—and their congregations—need to practice receptivity to that "kindling" which God provides when we make room for the attracting God. Preaching as spiritual direction attends to the life-giving rhythms of activity *and* receptivity, daily opening us to noticing God.

The Attracting God

As an itinerant preacher and retreat leader traveling to churches from Portland, Oregon, to St. Petersburg, Florida (and most points between), I am provided a rare glimpse into the broad spectrum of spiritual life among congregations and their members. I often inquire of retreatants, "Have you ever had a *transcendent* moment, in which the profound mystery at the heart of all life is revealed?" "Have you, in that moment, felt that God's presence is so utterly palpable that for one nano-second you glimpse the entire universe and its truths *and* your place within it, too?" Virtually every retreatant eagerly, *quickly* leans forward responding, "Yes!" I've watched as tens of dozens of congregations—of church folk—fill an entire wall (writing on huge sheets of paper) with transcendent experiences, listing everything from "the birth of my child" to "climbing the Great White Mountains" to "helping my dad die" to "walking on the beach" to "falling in love" to "last Sunday's choir anthem" and "my daughter's baptism" and "first communion." God lights the "spark" within us, powerfully, unforgettably in those fleeting, life-altering transcendent moments.

By way of contrast, when asked about their daily experiences of the *holy in the ordinary*, folks confess to a fantastic ability to *put God on hold*. Apparently it is one thing to *receive* a transcendent glimpse in an extraordinary moment—and another entirely to practice receptivity to God in the chaos of getting kids off to school and managing the unmanageable schedules and workloads. As they slam the minivan door shut and rush off into their daily grind, people experience a strong interior resistance to God's attempts to reach them.[24] It is a hard thing to accept, but practicing hospitality toward God in the daily mess of living is different from receiving God in a transcendent moment. For the daily revelations of God's love for us, we must *invite*, be hospitable to receiving God's efforts to kindle a spark within. This is precisely what spiritual direction does!

Retreatants report one place they cannot resist God's attempts at attracting them even in the hectic pace of life: creation. In the midst of even a momentary sight, sound, or smell—through sunrise, oak trees, thunderstorms, robins, snow, silky warm spring air, azalea blossoms, sunsets, beaches, plains, and rocks—retreatants experience a consistent openness to God. The writings of the

Desert Fathers are filled with stories mirroring what retreatants (some seven hundred years later) testify concerning their consistent attraction to God in nature. The well-educated Evagrius Ponticus, who in 382 left the great doctrinal battles in Constantinople for the desert, tells the following story:

> A certain member of what was then considered the circle of the wise once approached the just Antony and asked him: "How do you ever manage to carry on, Father, deprived as you are of the consolation of books?" His reply: "My book, sir philosopher, is the nature of created things, and it is always at hand when I wish to read the words of God."[25]

Whether a fourth-century Desert Father or a twenty-first-century soccer mom, outdoors human persons feel wooed by God and by the empty-yet-full, heart-deep pulse of creation. Emotions of peace, well-being, relaxation, at-one-ment emerge when we take notice of creation; although frequently, a sense of dis-ease, of being urged toward something—or a *call* to initiate change, growth, reconciliation—may also be evoked. More often than not, God's attempts to attract us through creation and its images are fulfilled.

Formation by Attraction

Theologian Margaret Miles writes that the experience of attraction is fundamental to human learning (and becoming) and thus essential to our relationship with God. She insists that image (whether a sunset *or* a painting of a sunset) is the beginning of insight.[26] Human beings, too, function as an attracting *image* capable of attracting others to God, as illustrated by Gabriel Marcel's observation (previously quoted): "I came to know God by loving someone in whom God dwelt." The phenomenon that both Miles and Marcel are describing is formation by attraction. When (more than twenty years ago now!) I asked Sittler about preaching—his response was that of telling the story of the crowd's amazed reaction to Jesus' outpouring love for Lazarus. Attracted by the image—the passion—they saw before them, the crowd wanted to "learn" this Jesus. The thinking of Sittler, Miles, and Marcel converge at the interplay between image, attraction, and human learning. Preaching at the convergence of this interplay is formation by attraction *and* it is preaching as spiritual direction.

Miles builds her theory of attraction in part on the theory of knowledge that Plato developed. As Miles points out,

> Plato's description of the development of knowledge is not a curriculum of subjects of progressive difficulty. It is, rather, a description of the way in which an act of vision [of the beautiful] . . . effectively gathers the energy requisite for initiating knowledge. Fascinated and delighted by the sight . . . gradually an ineffable awareness of 'the beautiful' grows . . .[27]

Plato praises the power of a beautiful image to attract the "learner," providing the intellectual intensity of *eros*, which, for Plato, is the necessary precondition of learning! Anyone who has stepped into Chartres Cathedral (or St. Patrick's in New York City, or any downtown cathedral) knows exactly what Miles and Plato mean. The shimmering sapphires, aquamarines, and iridescent golds of the stained-glass windows—punctuated by pulsing rose reds—cast hypnotic, spellbinding pools. We want to dive into them, *float* in them—as well as learn the stories and characters and personalities imaged in them. Bluntly put, we are attracted by what we see illumined before us.

Margaret Miles's work affirms what every visitor to Chartres knows, that *images* are a primary vehicle for engaging the process of attraction *and* essential to our relationship with God. Stained-glass windows—like the beauty of creation—attract us. Miles notes that the medieval, illiterate peasants who were attracted to and by the images in Europe's vast cathedrals full of stained-glass windows *learned* Bible stories through "reading" the windows.

Miles's affirmation of our natural capacity to respond—to pay attention—suggests an a priori openness to God. The human capacity to be open to (and to respond to) God is central to the theological understanding of the human person that Karl Rahner and other sacramental theologians developed, in which attraction is God's way of working within us. Miles's work suggests a profound theological anthropology of attention in which attraction is fundamental to preaching. Preachers, too, just like stained-glass windows and creation attract others to God's self. Just as in Sittler's example of the crowds that were moved by the power of Jesus' love for Lazarus, we, too, are moved by and drawn toward the God that we see *in* one another.

Sittler's observation itself *suggests* a model of preaching based on attraction, capable of awakening deep capacities for human love that all too often atrophy from inattention, grief, brokenness, and loss. Conspiring with hope that lies just beyond our brokenness, it is a lively homiletic that quite literally attracts us to the way of Jesus. Such preaching illumines a God that cannot be obtained, consumed, or manipulated but lived with, communed with; revealed intimately through community and relationships, in hilarity, grief, and baptism splashes. Open to risk and vulnerability, preaching as attraction rests on the certainty that individual well-being flourishes only when seeking the well-being of all, that *anthropos* can be *anthropos* only when securing the good of the whole cosmos.

Teresa of Calcutta, for example—as certainly as Chartres' windows—attracts. Teresa's beauty, though, is *not* like the aesthetic beauty of those stained-glass windows. It is instead Teresa's moral beauty that attracts us. Teresa's life totally given to God is intrinsically beautiful. And her attention to Christ "in his distressing disguise," as she put it, influences how we are attracted to God. Paul Tillich wrote that a saint is *not* a holy or pious person but that "Saints are persons who are transparent for the ground of being which is revealed through them. . . . Their being can become a sign-event for others."[28] Like a window, Teresa's life transparently reflects the light of Christ. We are attracted *through* her—to God. Preachers whose lives and very being are given to God attract us—like Teresa of Calcutta and those stained-glass windows—transparently conducting images and qualities that attract. Such preachers pay attention to God, cultivate receptivity for God, and their *sermons* are informed and shaped by attentiveness to God. So, too, the congregation draws closer to God, develops receptivity for God.

Attracting, Sacramental, Holy-in-the-Ordinary Ministers

The logic of formation by attraction as developed by Sittler, Rahner, and Miles (namely, that attraction is fundamental to human learning and growing) makes evident the sacramental importance of preaching as *attraction*. Further, it follows that a theory of preaching as spiritual direction adds "preacher" to the list of sacramental images through which the church attracts us to God, and consequently, through which God attracts us to one another—*and* to the mending of the world.[29] By speaking of the preacher as sacramental, I mean not that God magically speaks through the words of the sermon, or mystically through the person of the preacher. I mean, by contrast, that the preacher's own desire for God, nurtured in the disciplines of study, prayer, silence, and attentiveness, becomes tangible and powerful in the preached event. Thus, it becomes a *sign* of that fully-aliveness which Irenaeus called the "glory of God." The holy in the ordinary is revealed.

Saint Benedict was keenly aware of the sacramental aspects of attraction in guiding the growth and development of Christians. Benedict envisioned the monastery as a "school for the Lord's service" where the monks "run on the path of God's commandments," their hearts "overflowing with inexpressible delight of love."[30] Many a pastor's heart quickens with joy—and a simultaneous flush of envy—when first reading Benedict's vision for community life. No doubt, scant few of us, when seminarians, recognized Benedict's *monastic model* as an apt one for the congregations we would eventually serve. Granted, the distance between Benedict's sixth-century Roman Catholic monks and our twenty-first-century postmodern Protestant Christianity seems great. But Benedict's description of monks "overflowing with inexpressible delight of love" captures the fully aliveness and delight-filled attentiveness to God (*and* God's word) that pastors covet for their congregations. Benedict designs a sacramental model of leadership in his *Rule* (for monastic life), instructing the abbot to "keep in mind that he has undertaken the care of souls" and to remember "what he is and to what he is called."[31]

Benedict's awareness of the sacramental character of religious leadership is open to a rich diversity of gifts: educational leaders such as my teacher, Joseph Sittler, attract us by their insight and wisdom; activists like Daniel Berrigan and Martin Luther King Jr. attract us by their fierce hope and convict us to engage in prophetic critique and witness; the humility of a Teresa of Calcutta or Pope John XXIII draws us to living fully for others.

But it is not only the architecturally breathtaking Chartres Cathedral or the famous and physically strong that attract us to God. It would be difficult to find a church building less *attracting* (and more ordinary) than that of my childhood, Western Oaks Christian Church (Disciples of Christ) in Oklahoma City. Our "sanctuary" was a multipurpose (all purpose!) facility in which we not only worshiped, but potlucked, Sunday schooled, and recreated. Barn-like in architecture, with a flat pitch roof and brick and mortar walls, the windows were completely, crystal clear. At the conclusion of each Sunday's sermon our pastor imperatively exhorted us, "Look! Look clearly out these windows and *see* the needs of the world you depart now to serve." The holy in the ordinary.

I was the only kid among all my friends who had a church *without* stained-glass windows. I was also the only kid among all my peers whose pastor was a paraplegic. He and his brother contracted polio in the same week, though separated from one another by thousands of miles. That same week their father, a pharmacist, had received his first delivery of polio vaccine.

Those of us in Jerry Johnson's congregation were attracted to God *and* the world we were to "serve" through a man whose body was irretrievably broken, at least as most people viewed him. Attracting us most powerfully were Jerry's prayers. Jerry didn't merely *talk* about God—he *knew* God. And his prayers weren't pietistic pablum. Jerry demonstrated by example what Teresa of Avila, in her autobiography, urges upon all religious leaders, namely taking God as a friend: "No one ever took God for a friend that was not amply rewarded . . . for mental prayer is nothing else, in my opinion, but being on terms of friendship with God, frequently conversing . . . with [the One] who, we know, loves us."[32] Because, Teresa goes on to note, "Granting that we are always in the presence of God, it seems to me those who pray are in God's presence in a very different sense, for they, as it were, see that God is looking upon them; while others may be for days together without even once recollecting that God sees them."[33]

Sacramental pastors are moment by moment "recollecting" God's presence with them, cherishing the holy in the ordinary. For Teresa of Avila and other great spiritual luminaries of the past twenty centuries, prayer is ultimately a way of being receptive to the attracting God—as miraculous as the beating of our own heart. That's what our congregation overheard every Sunday as Jerry prayed. We saw before us a pastor intimate with God practicing *receptivity* toward God.

Teresa of Calcutta and those astounding widows at Chartres attract us in transcendent ways—ways that leave us breathless. We are attracted through awe. Then there's my pastor, Jerry. He was visibly broken, but his radiant, authentic love of God and compassion for the world's needs attracted us. Jerry's power wasn't physical; rather, it was unique and—it seemed to us—came straight from God. Jerry's congregants confessed to one another in whispers that in our dreams, Jerry walked, played basketball, and served communion with the strength of his own arms. But each morning, when dawn broke, we awoke to find our beloved pastor *still* restricted to that damned wheelchair, an ordinary man whose extraordinary friendship with God attracted us to God, too.

Although it is commonly recognized that word, table, baptism, wine, and bread are sacramental images that shape our imagination and awareness of God's presence, we often forget that these sacraments themselves are aspects of a deeper Christian *paidia*—the increasing capacity of the person (and congregation) to attend to the presence of God in the neighbor, the stranger, and even in the enemy. Pastors play a sacramental role in calling us to this deeper Christian schooling insofar as they shape our attention and capacity for seeking God always, in all ways. Such is the labor and delight of spiritual direction.

The preacher becomes sacramental: an embodied image through which God attracts. Such preachers—whose transparency guides others to God—are not a new phenomenon. George Herbert, rural Anglican poet and priest, was such a spiritual guide.

The Formational Pastor: George Herbert

A classic text that breathes life into the attracting and formation role of the preacher is George Herbert's *The Country Parson*.[34] Herbert's era, the post-Reformation period of the seventeenth century, was filled with constant disruption (and controversy) along with rapidly expanding knowledge—not unlike our post-modern era. Herbert argued that pastors should procure "attention by all possible art" to move their congregants toward intimacy with God.

Preachers need, Herbert writes (strikingly akin to Sittler's preacher-as-fire-alarm model), "a mountain of fire to kindle" their congregants.[35] Herbert, aware of the importance of formation by attraction, exhorted preachers to make certain their congregants "plainly perceive that every word [preached] is heart deep."[36] Herbert's great preaching (and poems) emerged from "attentiveness by all possible art" to prayer and to the congregations to which God had called him.

Herbert is perhaps best known for his shimmering poem, "The Call," later realized into a hymn by Ralph Vaughan Williams (1872–1958):

> Come, my Way, my Truth, my Life:
> Such a Way, as gives us breath:
> Such a Truth, as ends all strife:
> Such a Life, as killeth death.
>
> Come, my Light, my Feast, my Strength:
> Such a Light, as shows a Feast:
> Such a Feast, as mends at length:
> Such a Strength, as makes his guest.
>
> Come, my Joy, my Love, my Heart:
> Such a Joy as none can move:
> Such a Love as none can part:
> Such a Heart as joys in love.[37]

Herbert's words *attract* us to the God whom he intimately knows and transparently adores. Herbert—like those windows in Chartres—reveals God's light.

It wasn't all poetry and music for Herbert—he, too, knew the chronic demands of life in a local church, including a rigorous schedule of daily pastoral calls at the homes of congregants. Herbert patterned his life—as "country parson"—to interface deeply with the lives of his parishioners. He placed himself—as pastor—at the center of his congregants' lives in order to show them how God might become the center of *their* lives, ordering the entire "conduct of their existence" toward God.

Herbert walked *publicly* to church with his family each morning and evening to observe the reading of the Daily Offices. The effect Herbert's devotion to prayer had upon his parishioners was remarkable. Herbert's biographer, Izaak Walton, notes Herbert's example of morning and evening prayer "brought most of his Parishioners in the Neighborhood . . . to make a part of his Congregation twice a day."[38] Even those in the fields unable to attend Herbert's Daily Offices "would let their Plow rest when Mr. Herbert's Saints' Bell rung to Prayers, that they might also offer their devotions to God with him."[39]

Herbert's passionate conviction for "attention by all possible art" to *attract* congregants toward God demonstrates that pastoral leadership holds "no disjunction of word or sign, or of inner and outer, but a steadfast attempt to hold them together in a rich, precarious fullness."[40] Whether preaching or handling "holy things" during the Eucharist, the pastor's vocation is, first and foremost, that of formation by attraction. For Herbert, pastors, whose lives—and very being—are given to God transparently conduct images and qualities that attract other persons to God.

Preacher and Pastor as Spiritual Guide

Among the great luminaries of spiritual direction there are dramatic differences just like the differences that separate Evagrius Ponticus, St. Benedict, Teresa of Avila, Jerry Johnson, Teresa of Calcutta, and George Herbert. The "greats" are male *or* female; monk, priest, nun, *or* layperson; anchorite, scholastic, mystic, *or* saint; Egyptian, German, *or* North American; Cistercian, Dominican, Anglican, *or* Lutheran; ancient first-century up to the twenty-first. But far more amazing than the daunting differences between such spiritual guides are the characteristics they share in common. All of the spiritual greats were authentic, filled with self-knowledge, and an uncanny candor regarding both their capacities as well as their failings. They were devoted to religious confidants whose reliable self-feedback they sought. They were amazingly capable of "holding lightly" to their own self-will or will-to-power. Through careful attention to unhealthy or inordinate attachments they practiced a certain indifference to their own desires, which elicited in turn their increasing capacity for being drawn to God rather than being *driven* by anything other than God. This surfaced in them an exceptional capacity for compassion and spiritual freedom. They also had a gifted, no-nonsense understanding of their context, their faith communities, and the world.

Though their lives were centered in hope, they did not suffer from a naïve understanding of human anthropology—whether their own or that of their society or culture. Prayer was as a food to them—as necessary as eating, drinking, and sleeping. An utter devotion to and passion for their own spiritual formation and development was equally vital to them. For their own spiritual development they depended on the voices of past spiritual greats as well as the patterns and practices of their own faith communities—and they depended on the help of a *guide. They relied upon the art of spiritual direction and the skill of fine spiritual directors.* It wasn't always easy, though. Teresa of Avila, for instance, had repeated difficulties securing an adequate, trustworthy spiritual director who was not threatened by Teresa's own prodigious prayer life or by her many accomplishments as a *woman.*

Not only did the spiritual greats need guidance and spiritual direction. So, too, do ordinary, normal preachers and Christians populating churches throughout today's world. This insight became reinforced during my history of preaching doctoral course at Aquinas Institute of Theology in Saint Louis, for which each student was required to "inhabit" a master preacher through preaching a sermon in the style, theology, and manner of a great spiritual leader. I listened as my cohort exhibited the theology, the sociopolitical context, and the idiosyncrasies of their selected master teacher, whether Dietrich Bonhoeffer, Augustine, Mary Magdalene, or Fulton J. Sheen. Thunderstruck by how my colleagues' preaching took on a strength, a sureness, and a clarity of focus previously absent when relying upon merely their own voice and theology, I watched how each of us was changed by the simple act of "becoming" or "embodying" the spiritual master. This is a rich treasury to which we can lay claim: the religious authority of classical texts—including the "text" that literally *was* that spiritual master.

The characteristics of spiritual direction listed above are representative of authentic spiritual leaders—famous or not—across the ages. They are the characteristics Christian congregations seek, almost desperately, in their pastors and preachers in this disoriented, chaotic postmodern era. Preachers called to respond to the deep spiritual seeking of their congregants are preachers who seek to mend and tend their own spiritual development and to cultivate the characteristics exemplified in the persons mentioned above: putting down very deep roots, relying on the rich resources of the tradition of spirituality, and reappropriating its practices for our time.

Preaching as Spiritual Direction: A New Paradigm

Let me be "vehement as hell about the perfectly obvious," as Sittler would urge: North America scarcely needs another book on *how* to preach. The aforementioned constellation of homiletic luminaries (from John Broadus to Fosdick, Craddock, Buttrick, Troeger, and Long) brilliantly lights the path of any postmodern preacher seeking *how* to preach (as certainly as those ancient Magi were guided by their luminous star!) But again, this book's emphasis is the *aim* of preaching, not the *how*.

This book proposes a paradigm shift from the previous century's early preoccupation with preaching's purpose as *persuasion*—and its subsequent preoccupation with *explanation* and *communication*[41]—to a new paradigm of preaching as *guidance,* as spiritual formation for congregations *and* the individuals who comprise them.[42] This is not a completely new idea, having first been proposed in the twelfth century by Alan of Lille in his treatise, *The Seventh Rung*: "Preaching is an open and public instruction in faith and behavior, whose purpose is the forming of men . . . "[43]

What *is* new is this book's proposal that *spiritual direction* be the paradigm (and wisdom tradition) upon which formational preaching is built. Spiritual direction's fundamental concern is guidance, specifically guiding individuals and congregations toward noticing God, practicing receptivity with God, and seeking God always and *in* all ways. Guiding and shaping what is a lifelong process of formation is precisely why the discipline known as "spiritual direction" was developed.

Formational preaching is deeply incarnate—it is authentic, *real*—it wakes people up: like Jesus' tears for Lazarus shocked the crowds (as Sittler noted), astonishing them with his grief and love. As noted earlier, Irenaeus wrote, "The glory of God is a man fully alive."[44] Fully-aliveness is a distinctive characteristic of preaching as formation by attraction. Such preaching attracts and illumines souls, both of individuals and congregations, "awakening sleeping spirits" into fully-aliveness.

2 | FORMATIONAL VOICE-PRINTS

The blazing Oklahoma sun is pouring through the sanctuary windows of Western Oaks Christian Church, forming bright pools of light on the communion table. Organist Eleanor Neighbor sounds the opening notes of the prelude. Pastor Jerry Johnson sits in his wheelchair at the main entrance of the sanctuary, greeting each person as she or he enters, an elder standing beside him.

At the prelude's conclusion the elder guides Jerry's wheelchair up a long ramp to the chancel. Then, in one swift motion, the elder maneuvers Jerry's chair into the pulpit, simultaneously activating the pulpit's hydraulic lift. In moments Jerry—wheelchair, too, of course—is lifted up, visible to the congregation. From this "bird's eye view" of the congregation, Jerry unself-consciously bellows the words to the opening hymn, his out-of-tune voice amplified by the pulpit mike. We, the congregation, glance up from our hymnals, and we beam. Jerry's voice is our call to worship.

Voice Prints

Central among the attributes attracting congregants to Western Oaks Christian Church was Jerry's voice.[1] Gentle, lilting, sometimes playful, his preaching voice mirrored the soft-spoken voice he employed in daily conversation. Beyond Jerry's distinctive physiological voice-print, the congregation was attracted by the voice-print of his spirituality, audibly palpable in the compassionate, vulnerable timbre of his voice, perhaps as a result of polio or the consequent challenges of living and pastoring as a paraplegic. Intellectually speaking, Jerry's voice-print was shaped by Scripture, psychology, science, literature, and liberal theology. As certainly as the Holy Spirit drove Jesus into the desert, the desire for Jerry Johnson's voice drove the congregation to church each Sunday.

Each human voice is "demonstrably unique . . . as clear and definitive as a finger print."[2] And each preacher—whether Jerry Johnson, or Martin Luther King Jr., or Barbara Brown Taylor—indelibly carries the voice-print of the preacher who shaped him or her![3]

Alan of Lille (c. 1182–1202), in his revolutionary treatise *The Seventh Rung*, left a profound voice-print on the development of preachers and homiletic theory. Allan posited the aim of preaching to be that of *formation*, noting "preaching is an open and public instruction in faith and behavior, whose purpose is the forming of men . . ."[4] Lille, through emphasizing preaching's aim as *formation*, initiated an important shift in homiletics, forsaking "one key element in the classical definition of oratory, namely persuasion, and instead speaks pastorally of 'formation' as the goal of Christian preaching."[5]

Homiletically speaking, then, the voice-prints of our forebears have implications for how we engage our authority to preach, as well as for how (and what) we think regarding preaching's aim, and the sources to which we turn for wisdom. Preachers-to-be and congregants are *formed* by such voices.

The current self-understanding of the homiletic task, for example, has been dominated by the indelibly unique voice-print of Fred Craddock. In his book *As One Without Authority*,[6] Craddock cleverly utilized irony in the title to criticize deductive authoritarian and dogmatic models of preaching in favor of a more inductive, imaginative, dialogical, and existentially authentic method of preaching. Craddock sought to refocus the notion of pastoral authority for the North American context of the 1970s, his main concern being that of "getting the sermon *heard*."[7] The increasingly secularized North American culture in the decades following the publication of *As One Without Author-ity* has experienced the weakening of both pastoral leadership generally and homiletic power more specifically. Though the title of Craddock's book was intentionally ironic, it has regret-tably become an apt description of the diminishment of pastoral authority. Though my seminary students, for example, dem-onstrate a profound commitment both to the church and to their call into ordained ministry, they simultaneously resist self-identifying as religious leaders, regardless of denominational affiliation. This apprehension at the heart of pastoral authority affects the pastor's capacity to lead congregations and to preach effectively.

Formational Preaching

Today's North American seminarians derive their religious self-identity primarily from *au courant* metaphors such as wounded healer, counselor, therapist, C.E.O., and friend, rather than from specifically religious Christian traditions of spiritual direc-tor, spiritual guide, or wisdom figure. That pastors do not envi-sion their religious authority as spiritual guide or wisdom figure affects not only pastoral leadership, but also the very subject mat-ter of preaching. Spiritual instruction, exhortation, or illumi-nation—in the face of the spiritually parched landscape of our postmodern culture—remains a rare eventuality in North Ameri-can sermons.

It would be difficult, for example, for any of us to name a teenager (or young adult) *not* struggling with very real issues of vocational discernment, yet North American mainline pulpits have echoed with a resounding silence on such critically impor-tant issues as: (1) discerning one's call to a committed relation-ship, to marriage, and to parenting (or *not*); (2) exploring one's vocation (be it to a profession, a trade, or a fine art); (3) discover-ing the importance of one's *avocation* and its life-giving creativ-ity; (4) processing each person's call to ministry (both clergy and lay); and, ultimately, (5) growing toward spiritual freedom in God through Christ. In over a decade of listening to student sermons none has preached on issues of vocation, discernment, or forma-tion; nor has a student sermon utilized a classic text of spiritual formation (though psychological and sociological experts are quoted authoritatively *ad infinitum*).

Twenty centuries of Christian spiritual instruction on the intricacies of spiritual growth and development, including discernment of vocation (from the Desert Fathers and Mothers, the *Rule* of St. Benedict, the autobiography of Teresa of Avila, Ignatius of Loyola, right on up through Thomas Merton, Simone Weil, and Evelyn Underhill) are relatively unknown by theologically educated pastors. Consequently, these vital, life-giving texts remain virtually unused and untouched by North American preachers.[8]

Just as exegesis of Scripture does not mean that one retreats to a first-century view of the world, so attention to the classics of Christian spirituality does not mean that one retreats to a fifth- or sixteenth-century view of the world. Rather, renewed attention to these rich texts and to their vocabulary and practices of Christian formation can help provide an appropriate and distinctive approach to pastoral authority. In these texts, one finds rich and complex religious imagery, a focus on communal formation, and practices of prayerful and theological discernment that can still move us and provoke us toward a creative analogical imagination. Parker Palmer, for example, retrieves both the monastery's commitment to community and its disciplines of prayer and work as a way to reimagine congregations as formational communities. Retrieving the best from that historic, communal tradition necessarily includes attending to the range of its spiritual wisdom, such as (but not limited to) the Ignatian, Teresian, Franciscan, Benedictine, and Cistercian models of Christian spirituality. All work together to connect the Christian tradition's focus on formation with the needs and deep desires of contemporary Christians.

How is it that today's preachers do not understand preaching's aim to be that of formation, and why have preachers virtually dismissed over twenty centuries of classic, Christian texts of spiritual wisdom as if inadvisable sources for preaching? These questions require a return to the most influential preacher of the early twentieth century, Harry Emerson Fosdick (1878–1969).[9]

Formational Voice-Prints: Fosdick

Harry Emerson Fosdick's method and voice were, figuratively speaking, the D.N.A. responsible for the formation of pastors, preaching, and congregations for decades—up through today. But Fosdick, too, emerged in the midst of an *inherited* homiletic landscape, the contours of which were born virtually alongside him, namely: Austin Phelps's *Theory of Preaching*[10] and John Broadus's *A Treatise on the Preparation and Delivery of Sermons.* Both these textbooks were employed in the education of preachers until the 1950s (long into Fosdick's preaching career), with Broadus's text, as Mountford points out, being "widely considered to be the most successful American textbook on preaching of all time with forty editions published between 1870 and 1896 alone."[11] In particular, these texts helped shift homiletic theory from persuasion to explanation. The development of the modern sermon as explanation arose in response to a new anxiety, namely, that of negotiating the intellectual power of modern science without falling into either rigid fundamentalism or vapid secularism. The purpose of the sermon was to help the congregation to reconcile Christian tradition with a modern, scientific worldview.

Unsurprisingly, in Fosdick's era, when a primary burden of the preacher's work included negotiating a peace between science and religion, preachers gained their authority by mastering secular education, by demonstrating through knowledge and propositional logic how religious teaching could get along with such a newly understood phenomenological world. This emphasis on secular education was initially introduced into preaching when Phelps advised: "A thoroughly trained preacher is first a man, at home among men: he is then a scholar, at home in libraries."[12] Such a "thoroughly trained preacher" and "scholar, at home in libraries" was *not* reading Desert Fathers and Mothers, or mystics while there. He was reading of the latest scientific discoveries, studying concepts surfacing from the "new" disciplines of psychology and sociology, and following current philosophical debates. He was, above all, pursuing knowledge that was relevant to his time. The self-identity and authority of the modern preacher were derived primarily from the pastor's *superior* [secular] *knowledge.*[13] Monasticism, mysticism, and desert wisdom were not understood as valid wisdom from which a modern preacher might choose to construct a modern sermon. Mysticism and the classic writings of Western Christian spirituality would have been dismissed as magical (in opposition to science and its "facts"). For the modern worldview, humanity had superseded such unscientific ways of perceiving the world, as had the modern scholar-preacher.

It was in the midst of the unfolding of this modern context that Fosdick's preaching model emerged. It is difficult to overestimate his influence on the development of mainline preaching (and United States' congregations) in the second half of the twentieth century. His sermons were broadcast over The National Vespers Radio Hour and Fosdick's voice-print "year after year reached millions of people."[14] After World War II Fosdick's method of preaching as pastoral counseling was adopted throughout America's mainline, liberal pulpits and "the American people came to accept psychology as the new orthodoxy"[15] within the larger rubric of liberal theology. Like other historical figures who indelibly altered a form by elevating it to new heights (for example, Shakespeare's mastery of the medieval English sonnet and J. S. Bach's brilliant exploitation of baroque dance forms), Fosdick elevated the modern sermon form. Fosdick's accomplishment was the result not only of his prodigious talent but also of a rich set of homiletic challenges posed by modernity: sociological, intellectual, and theological challenges, including science and technology, and existentialism.

Harry Emerson Fosdick, America's "most prominent liberal Protestant preacher when religious liberalism knew its finest hour," pioneered and nurtured the late-modern notion of preaching as "counseling."[16] Psychology and secular wisdom resourced this model of preaching. In his sermon, "The Real Point of Conflict Between Science and Religion," Fosdick brilliantly demonstrated the modern sermon's preoccupation with science and human progress while simultaneously revealing his personal context in a subtle yet public way:

What areas of human need science has met in my lifetime! When I was born, Edison was thirty-one years old; Sigmund Freud was twenty-two; Henry Ford was fifteen; Charles

Steinmetz, thirteen; Madam Curie, eleven; Orville Wright, seven; Marconi, four; Einstein, minus one.[17]

We have here a preacher-scholar who interprets his own life within the span of modern inventors, psychologists, scientists, and physicists whose lives and work Fosdick envisions as dovetailing with his own. In Fosdick's energetic words one can hear—like an engine humming—the liberal theologians' profound admiration for human striving and becoming, its unrestrained confidence in science and human invention. Himself shaped by modernity's great figures, Fosdick both inherited and shaped the voice-print of liberal theological preaching. Absent from this set of modern emphases was any sense of indebtedness to a specifically Christian past and its traditions, its wisdom figures, and its concern with spiritual formation. There is little of George Herbert in Fosdick's romancing of the modern spirit, even less of the Desert Fathers or Mothers or the writings of monastics, mystics, or reformers.

Fosdick launched his new model (and a new era) of preaching with an article in *Harper's Magazine*, July 1928, called "What Is the Matter with Preaching?":

> Every sermon should have for its main business the solving of some problem—a vital, important problem, puzzling minds, burdening consciences, distracting lives—and any sermon which thus does tackle a real problem, throw even a little light on it and help some individuals practically to find their way through it cannot be altogether uninteresting.[18]

As O. C. Edwards points out, "The method of preaching [Fosdick] recommended in the article has been variously described as 'life-situation' or 'problem-centered,' but [Fosdick] referred to it as the 'project method'."[19] Call it what you will, it is preaching founded on psychology and pastoral counseling; science is the authoritative voice, and the "hurting" individual the primary focus.

The pressures and influences of the larger cultural context in which preaching occurs cannot be underestimated. For example, at the height of modernity higher criticism and science strode into the seminaries, divinity schools, and pulpits of the United

States of America. The long arm of psychology and Sigmund Freud arrived as well. In a gradual evolution, pastoral formation, preaching, and theology were influenced by modern, psychologically constructed models. Eventually these pastoral counseling and psychology-based models became the cornerstone of preaching and pastoral care within mainline Protestant seminaries and churches. Liberal theology's naïve belief in the foundational goodness of the human person—deeply influenced by psychology— also came to the fore. These influences came together in the person of Fosdick in the context of modern preaching.

Edmund Linn aptly describes the fundamental problem that Fosdick's homiletic aimed to solve: "If religion seems to such people—or seemed to the people of Fosdick's congregations—to have a valid place in this cosmos, it must be rational and intelligible. These people need to be convinced that both scientific and Christian truth can contribute to their fulfillment as persons."[20] There was a secondary aim, too, pointedly expressed by Fosdick, "We need more sermons that try to face people's real problems with them, meet their difficulties, answer their questions, confirm their noblest faiths and interpret their experiences in sympathetic, wise and understanding cooperation."[21] With this forceful statement, Fosdick established the secondary aim in modern preaching: pastoral counseling. As Linn observes astutely: "By application of the principles of personal counseling to preaching, the counseling sermon becomes no less a technique for the transformation of persons than actual counseling itself."[22] The preacher is exhorted to enter the pulpit "expecting that lives will be made over, families will be saved, young people will be directed into wholesome paths, potential suicides will become happy and useful members of the society, and doubters will become vibrant believers."[23]

While Fosdick's preaching was biblically based, the hermeneutic "need" driving biblical interpretation was that of negotiating peace between science, modernism, and prehistorical critical models of biblical interpretation. In modern-era preaching, such as Fosdick's, the Bible retained its fundamental, formative role—but biblical conversation partners (homiletically speaking) included "scientific experts" and "modern scholars."

Under Fosdick's brilliant rhetorical guidance preaching became a rational, problem-based, problem-solving project with modern psychology as its foundation. The progress of individual well-being became preaching's fundamental aim. Neither the formational aspect of congregational preaching nor the broader context of the congregation's missional role toward God's justice and mercy in the world were primary concerns.[24] As has been noted earlier, specifically Christian traditions, wisdom figures, and formational concerns were utterly absent, their authority displaced in an effort toward validating science and modern scholarship *within* Christian preaching.

In the "Fosdickian project," the exegesis of individual psyches, temperaments, and personalities received a level of attention that was, historically speaking, given quite exclusively to biblical texts. In his sermon "The Great Hours of a Man's Life," Fosdick exegeted his personal experience employing the power of modern psychology to reveal liberal theology's ethic of personal progress:

> One of my boyhood's recollections is my father dealing with me when I was in a bad temper, "Where's Harry?" he would say, and I would answer, "Why, here he is." And he would say to me, "NO! You are not Harry. Harry is lost. Go find him. I want Harry!" So, catching his meaning, I would wander off through the house, getting myself under control until, returning, I could face him again, saying, "I've found him. Here he is." Thus my father said to me, as a child, *what modern psychology is saying now*—that we are not just one self, but varied selves, high and low, good and bad, and that the art of life is to identify oneself with one's best self, and believe and be what the best self affirms.[25]

According to Fosdick's method, sermons should "suggest rather than command, explain rather than exhort, and discuss rather than dictate."[26] We see here the reaction against didactic, expository preaching, and we see also the genius Fosdick developed for "exegeting" individuals within the congregation. This, for its time, was a thoroughly modern, effective model of preaching, particularly as a response to the premodern didactic sermons whose purpose was salvation. Yet Fosdick's model with its wholehearted embrace of modern assumptions and conventions was not without consequences.

The Problem with Preaching as Pastoral Counseling

When pastoral problem solving became the foundational model for both pastor and preacher, the very curriculum and landscape of theological education was altered. Pastoral care centers sprang up next door to seminaries where a modern conceptualization of care of the soul was practiced. This post-World War II conceptualization of the "care of the soul" collapsed into a virtually exclusively psychological understanding of the human person, in which the language of the "self" eclipsed mention of the "soul." The church's classic Christian traditions, texts, and practices—as well as critical interpretations of those historical landscapes—lay discarded, disdained.

Finally, some scholars sounded alarms, such as practical theologian and Disciple of Christ scholar Don Browning who, in 1976, wrote: "Pastoral care and counseling must be able to show what is 'Christian' and 'pastoral' about what the minister does when he offers his services."[27]

> Nothing more clearly indicates the church's lack of direction and general identity confusion than this penchant for borrowing uncritically and with almost reckless enthusiasm for the newest technique that attracts the attention of the popular mind.
>
> The free and ready utilization by modern pastoral care and counseling . . . leaves the impression that larger ecclesiastical and cultural contexts are somehow neutral concerning its assumptions and procedures. Insights from psychoanalysis, from the therapies of Carl Rogers, Eric Berne, Fritz Perls, and B. F. Skinner, can be readily borrowed and employed with breathtaking rapidity. Group approaches, individual approaches, depth approaches, marathon techniques, encounter experiences and sensitivity training have been quickly adopted. . . . What is astounding about this phenomenon is not so much the willingness to experiment but rather the almost total lack of critical reflection on the question of compatibility.
>
> *How do these various techniques and theories relate to the larger goals implicit in the church's ministry?*[28]

Yet, in the late-modern era, when science, technology, and the myth of progress were still gods, warnings like Browning's were largely ignored.[29] Practices such as spiritual direction were suspect because of their lack of scientific foundational principles and proof of their efficacy. They also were little known by the Protestant mainline community, a lasting residue of the Reformation's unintended yet negative consequence. Ancient wisdom had a whiff of unseemliness—theologically fuzzy, dealing with the affective and mysterious, suspiciously papist. Dialectical theologian Reinhold Niebuhr, for example, was representative of this modern skepticism regarding anything "mystical."

When mainline Protestant preachers adopted, too uncritically, that post-World War II model of Protestant preaching which had explanation (rather than persuasion) as its aim, liberal theology was preached in concert with a therapeutic or counseling model of preaching. The "wisdom" texts (extracanonically speaking) referenced by preachers emerged entirely from modernity's project, particularly psychology and science. The popular journal *Psychology Today* and sociological treatises like Robert Putnam's *Bowling Alone*, for example, still receive remarkable press in current student preaching. Classic, historical Christian texts of spiritual formation and wisdom with their nuanced understanding of the complexities of the human soul are abandoned.[30]

As psychology's influence grew more predominant in U.S. culture throughout the 1960s and 1970s, mainline denominations began requiring Clinical Pastoral Education (C.P.E.) for pastors. Courses in family systems, pastoral care for the congregation, and developmental psychology became common curriculum choices for ministers in training. Robert Cueni, former president of Lexington Theological Seminary, anecdotally notes that when he graduated from Christian Theological Seminary with a Master of Divinity degree he had thirty-five hours credit in psychology—and "not a single preaching course."

In their writings on pastoral care, pastors and theologians claimed to speak for, and out of, the pivotal genre of Christian discourse known as the care of souls, even as they virtually abandoned all of the classic Christian texts in favor of the new psychological models. Pastors thus began to envision themselves as therapeutic listeners. Pastors were now "therapists" who approached their congregations as a group of discrete "hurting and broken" individuals in need of healing.[31]

As Browning had noted, many aspects of the various approaches to psychology (for example, Transactional Analysis, Gestalt, as well as Rogerian, Freudian, and Jungian models) could be "basically useful at the level of increasing a person's ability to be free to act."[32] Yet, the freedom to act and self-actualization, while helpful, are not to be confused with the self-knowledge, spiritual freedom, and relationship to God's presence. Further, the basis of a pastor's *religious* authority to preach—rather than the authority of "pastor as scholar"—was diminished during the modern era. Currently, and dishearteningly, a pastor's *religious* authority is seldom visited (volitionally or vocationally) either in student sermons or in class discussions.

Unforeseen Negative Consequences of Preaching as Counseling

The modern counseling model of preaching brought great strengths to the pulpit. We learned that congregational history and experience could and must be interpreted, as well as Scripture. Human experience became a palpable source for investigation and proclamation from the pulpit. As Thomas Long notes, preachers engaging this model of preaching gave "attention to the inner dynamics of preaching."[33] But there also are unforeseen negative consequences visited upon the individuals and congregations shaped by this model. Some of the consequences are fairly insidious, though clearly never intended to be such by Fosdick or other pastors. The four consequences that I discuss and develop, while not comprising an exhaustive list, identify and clarify several among the operative shortcomings of preaching as counseling, all of which may be subsumed under a paradigmatic umbrella of modernity.

1. It shrinks the grid of Christianity to fit modernity's project.

• *Creating a naïve confidence in objective reason.* Douglas John Hall, in *Thinking the Faith*, rightly argues that the Enlightenment tended toward an overly optimistic view of the human project and that, over time, this optimism came to function as a kind of cultural boosterism which (understandably) avoided grappling with shadows of suffering.[34] The mistaken cultural optimism lay in the confidence that modern science could grasp the world objectively, and that experts could, in turn, apply that objective knowledge to solve human problems. Drawing on that same confidence, the therapeutic model's preoccupation with diagnosis inevitably treated both the person seeking the cure, and that person's suffering, as "object" (a technical problem to be solved).

Paul Tillich, in his *Systematic Theology*, alerted us to the difference between "technical reason" and "ontological reason."[35] While the former has been enormously helpful in the modern period, sharpening our capacities for critical analysis and aiding our understanding of both historical life and the natural world, it does not exhaust the nature of human reason. Ontological reason, by which we engage in wonder at the mystery of Being and ask about the meaning of our existence, both personally and collectively, moves in a different direction and with a different orientation than its technical partner. Ontological reason, for Tillich, does not solve the mystery of existence, but encourages and enables us to enter into and participate more fully in it. Tillich's distinction continues to prove helpful for recognizing that the attempt to understand the Christian practices of preaching and pastoral care in terms of the "technical" strategies of modern psychology is bound to be too constrictive.

Other thinkers of the neoorthodox school, such as Reinhold Niebuhr, for example, and later Langdon Gilkey, criticized the optimism of modern, liberal culture and specifically liberal theology as utterly naïve. These dialectical theologians argued that so-called objective reason tended to follow the cultural, political, and institutional self-interests of various groups.[36] Reason, far from being objective or disinterested, these theologians argued, frequently functioned as a means of self-deception, blinding both the self and the community to the abiding problematic of human sin. Claims of objective reason, they warned, function as a form of denial, blinding both the self and the community to its moral obligations. It took time, however, for voices such as Niebuhr's and Gilkey's to be heard, not only in theological circles, but in local churches as well.

• *Treating individual Christians like clients.* In the meantime, homileticians such as Fosdick had begun to understand both church life and preaching in terms of the problem-solving techniques of modern psychology, with the pastor in the role of local expert. In the preaching-as-pastoral-counseling model, pastors approach their congregations as a group of discrete individuals: clients. Community organizer John McKnight, in his insightful chapter "Professionalized Service and Disabling Help," argues that professionalized therapeutic culture has been disastrous for life in the public square generally.[37] Rather than a community full of *vocations* in need of *direction*, the congregation is viewed as a set of individualized and private clients, whose tithes and offerings constitute a fee for the professionalized services of the pastor. Preaching becomes a therapeutic message to a group of hurting individuals in a hurting world rather than a formational message toward shaping the body of Christ that we are to become. Pastors and congregants take their eyes off the work of God that is ours to do in the world. Paradoxically, while we gaze introspectively into ourselves in a psychologically informed model (rather than that of the Christian wisdom tradition's seeking of self-knowledge) we are distracted from the vision God asks us to behold.

• *Reducing conceptualizations of God to that of the "fixer."* When the human condition becomes a problem to be solved for which science and psychology offer the cure, is there any need for God? Or—as in the case of many late-modern Protestants nurtured on the counseling model of preaching—might God be reduced to a "fix-it god" that is to be worshipped or placated? Theologically speaking, the crisis of therapeutic preaching becomes one of idolatry rather than that of unbelief. Ultimately, the fix-it, problem-solving approach presumes the fixable nature of human beings rather than their interdependence with the Divine Mystery at the heart of all being.

• *Transforming churches into can-do, solution-oriented chambers of commerce.* Churches imbued with the Fosdickian approach to preaching tend to exhibit a kind of can-do optimism and solutionism in their life together that papers over or avoids the real suffering in a situation or community.[38] Solution-oriented churches focus their attention inward: upon themselves and "getting our needs met" rather than on God's insatiable thirst for kin-dom love and justice—and thus abdicate playing anything but a private role in bringing about such a kin-dom. In the problem-solving model, people approach every situation—*even their spiritual lives*—in light of a solution, or product, to be produced. But the fruits of the Spirit cannot be consumed and harvested so much as *cultivated*. Rather than objectifying spiritual gifts as products, we must understand them as a lifelong process that may be lived into, not so much achieved. These gifts of the Spirit are elusive and consistently slip through our grasp, as intangibles always do. While Julian of Norwich assured us that "all will be well," her confidence lay not in our ability to produce solutions, but in the elusiveness and beneficent presence of God.[39]

The problems of rationalization, self-centeredness, and professional objectification, which we find in a solution-oriented church, participate in the cultural misadventure of consumerism. The transformation of the American economy from one that at the turn of the twentieth century largely produced *things* to one that at the beginning of the twenty-first century largely produces *services* has been astounding. The new service-based economy's need for ever-new human "neediness" that can then be met or *solved*[40] by purchasing the latest fix, the newest technology, or the most recent self-help book, has contributed greatly to the church's bondage to the therapeutic model. Finally, the solution-oriented, problem-solving approach to preaching is responsible, I suspect, for much of the burnout in pastors and lay ministers. We have been so busy trying to solve problems with technical solutions that we have no time to nurture our longing for God or God's longing for justice in the world. As long as we approach systemic issues as problems to be solved, rather than as a lifelong process that is to be engaged corporately, we are increasingly easily discouraged, weak hearted, and (paradoxically) less likely to take on seemingly overwhelming issues like poverty, violence, racism, sexism, classism, and heterosexism.

• *Viewing our spiritual lives as problems to be fixed (or solved).* Spiritual director Margaret Guenther wryly notes the "assumption that everything is, in principle, fixable" is a myth.[41] Spiritual direction stands in direct contrast with North America's myth of progress, presuming instead the "un-fixability" in human life and institutions! According to Guenther, "It's about mortality. It's about love. It's about things that can't be fixed" but which can be lived into, *deeply*, with God's help.[42]

In my nine years of hearing student preachers, virtually every sermon—though not always intentionally—can be categorized within Fosdick's therapeutic, preaching-as-counseling, problem-solving model. Problem-solving preaching remains the predominant strand of today's preaching's D.N.A. The Sufi mystics have a story in which some fish were anxiously swimming around looking for water. As they swam their anxiety became more and more escalated. One day they met a wise fish and asked him, "Where is the sea?" The wise fish answered: "If you would stop swimming . . . you would discover that you are already in the sea." Like the fish swimming in the water of the Sufi legend,[43] mainline preachers in the United States have swum around so long in the waters of the therapeutic model that we no longer recognize it. As professor of preaching I have heard an endless variety of sermons that "fix things." Sermons that fix the church, fix sin, fix the congregation, fix the enemy (whether conservative or liberal), fix the budget, fix the denomination. But when it comes to intractable tragic suffering and war, poverty and violence—that which is beyond problem solving and which is by its nature insoluble—my students keep silent because they have inherited their preaching D.N.A. from Fosdick and the modern project's presupposition that everything in life is fixable.

Once, when making a retreat with Father Daniel Berrigan, I was impressed by his devotion to the daily, moment-to-moment labor of being faithful to God—particularly in light of the very real fact that as a result of Berrigan's activity *absolutely nothing was fixed*.[44] During the retreat, a young man asked Berrigan: "Why do you persist in denting massive nuclear warheads with a few ineffective blows from a hammer then marking them with human blood? . . . Nothing's changed. Why keep doing it?" Berrigan looked quizzically at the person—as if confused by the "effectiveness question" posed by the young man—and responded: "Well, that's what we do as Christians. We repeat ourselves. Regardless of outcome. A voice crying in the wilderness. It's not a story; it's a job description." It was as if it had never occurred to Berrigan that a faithful person might presume or *hope* to be effective, to "fix things." Berrigan continued: "But we can *live* the question, over and over again: is this [current state of affairs] what God intends?"

2. It elevates psychological "experts" to authoritative status regarding the "self" while ignoring classic Christian wisdom texts and traditions regarding the development of the "soul."

A second consequence of preaching as counseling lies within its abdication of therapeutic wisdom traditions within the history of Christian thought and practice, while treating secular psychological models as "gospel." It has been only very recently that scholars, such as theologian David Tracy, have begun to reappropriate such wisdom texts. Tracy's language of "retrieval" enables us, by way of example, to engage the textual tradition of pastoral and spiritual formation, reaching back to the Desert Fathers and Mothers and into the classic writings of communal leaders such as Augustine, Benedict, Gregory the Great, Francis and Clare, Teresa of Avila, as well as attention to more modern texts by Bonhoeffer, Merton, Weil, King, and others. These teachers, texts, and traditions provide not only resources but also vocabulary for a consistent sense of "orientation" and "direction" in our personal and congregational lives. Tracy would include such teachers and their texts as "classic."[45] Although some authors, such as Parker Palmer,[46] have sought to retrieve the best insights of monasticism to inform and confront our own struggles to form disciplined and publicly engaged Christian communities, sermon reference to the wisdom of the Desert Fathers and Mothers, the mystics, martyrs (as already mentioned) remain tragically rare.

Like jewels, the treasures of Christian spirituality and their shimmering wisdom are waiting to be mined—to be reappropriated—in our preaching, teaching, and church life. While these texts, prayer disciplines, and pastoral traditions will need to be reinterpreted in light of today's vastly different circumstances, we must first acknowledge their claim upon us. Far from ignoring such texts, they are incandescent enough to light our way in this postmodern time of disorientation. For example, Teresa of Avila's autobiography is chock-full of advice and tips for developing and maintaining community well-being. I remember being drawn up short as a young pastor—who preferred certain members of her congregation over others—when I read Teresa's advice in *The Way of Perfection*: "All must be friends with each other, all must love each other, be fond of each other, and help each other."[47] Teresa goes on to caution against either "excess or defect of love" toward those in our community. Granted, hers was a professed religious community, but the wisdom remains transparent to postmodern pastors.

When, in the progression of modern discourse, the "self" and the psychological understanding of human psyche replaced the "soul," the shift tended to objectify and universalize the human (and the natural). It was during modernity's shift from "soul" to "self" that preachers abandoned classic spiritual texts. Unintentional reductions of human nature in the modern disciplines of psychology and economics to self-interest or to unconscious drive left little room for the ennobling of the spirit or soul. The modern emphasis upon the logic of exchange in virtually all social sciences (which has found its way into our preaching) discounts the possibility and reality of "gift."[48]

By contrast, the classics of Western Christian spirituality hold open the possibility of deep existential renewal and transformation, correcting the reductionist tendencies of modernity. Imaginative impulse and the envisioning of creative, self-giving, gifting lives are typical among the classic texts of Christian spirituality. The mystics' lives—and particularly their dynamic understanding of prayer as an alternative and relational form of discourse—resist the modern conceptualization of a dynamics of exchange in favor of that of purpose-filled lives of hope, communion, discipline, and self-giving.

Modern emphases upon rationality in science and the social sciences (including not only psychology but the historical criticisms of both Scripture and tradition) have been fruitful for "understanding" the world and the world of Christian tradition (both its strengths and failings). But, ultimately, these rationalities have not helped us orient our lives in profound and purposeful ways. For that, our preaching must turn to the wise voices of the geniuses of Christian formation and spirituality that span the centuries.[49]

Renewed attention to these rich texts and to their practices of Christian formation can help provide a basis for imagining an appropriate and distinctive approach to pastoral authority. In these texts, one finds rich and complex religious imagery, a focus on communal formation, and practices of prayerful and theological discernment that move us, and provoke us toward a creative analogical imagination. Retrieval of the monastic commitment to community and its disciplines of prayer and work are helpful templates for reconstruing congregations as communities of honest, trusting discourse that encourage a range of spiritual disciplines. The Christian tradition's focus on formation—when properly reimagined and reappropriated—forms an oasis of possibilities for meeting deep desires of contemporary Christians for encountering the presence of God.

It might be asked, "Why should a Christian preacher consider extracanonical sources of wisdom (such as Desert Father and Mothers, mystics, martyrs, and reformers) beyond the life, ministry, death, and resurrection of Jesus as revealed in the New Testament?" Jesus' teachings, sayings, and parables deal principally with ethical and social issues of justice and mercy. Even though they seem to function on an instructional level. the words of Jesus do not actually guide us formationally in *how* to love God with our "whole heart, mind, soul, and strength" as individual Christians, nor do they guide us in how to practice our faith *communally*. While certainly, for example, Jesus instructed us to "love one another" we cannot simply *will* ourselves to it—nor, apparently, be *inspired* to it with brilliant exegetical skills and scintillating preaching, though Paul did his very best to accomplish precisely that in his mission churches! In the end we need patterns, practices, and methods to guide us in our interaction with one another and shape our interior landscapes toward God. Desert Fathers and Mothers knew— and the early monastic Abbas, too—there is a gap to be bridged between Jesus' instructions to human persons and our capacities to live into Jesus' exhortations and expectations.

3. It mistakes "understanding" for healing and substitutes "pain relief" for spiritual growth and engagement.

Within the therapeutic, psychological model is the implied notion that understanding brings healing. That my mother called me the "light of her life," that I am the middle daughter of three girls, that I was a gifted child in the midst of an Oklahoma culture of football with its aggressive suspicion of learning and of the intellectual life, affected me certainly. And I am grateful to therapy for understanding how certain causes and effects operated within my sphere of development. In fact, it is difficult to conceive my life without this therapeutic context. But in the end these rationalities did not help me to orient my life in profound, purposeful ways. All the understanding in the world therapeutically did not give me a solid rock on which to build a life. Only theologically, through the education (*paidia*) of Christian "school"—church, prayer, mystics, my spiritual director, and spiritually alive mentors and preachers—have I grown into my human becoming, something therapy with its attendant gifts of understanding was unable to accomplish.

The therapeutic aspect of relieving symptoms of pain and suffering has had a long and negative impact on our theologies and our spiritual lives. Inarguably, psychological models of various sorts have provided ways for people to face serious problems and suffering with courage and hope, particularly in the midst of mental and emotional crises. In their attempt to treat a mental/emotional disorder, either to cure it or to medicate it, those therapies seek to alleviate suffering of mind and body. They aim to return us to ourselves as individual, private persons. While this is certainly a worthy endeavor, and while psychological therapies and psychotropic pharmacological therapies have their place in contemporary understandings of mental healing, the wholesale acceptance of modern psychology's assumptions of human personhood has been deeply problematic in Christian theology. By accepting uncritically the modern project of fixing human suffering, Christians have, along with the rest of North American culture, been persuaded that suffering is something that can be (and should be) avoided, and doing so is virtually always a good thing.[50] Yet, as the optimism of modernity's problem-solving ethos fades, and as confidence in its various modes of technical reason turns to profound moral dismay, postmodern people, Christian and not, are discovering again that not all forms of human suffering can be or should be eradicated.

In pointed contrast to modernity's ethos of optimistic boosterism, Douglas John Hall has described the peculiar North

American *problematique* in terms of avoidance and flight from suffering. Opting too easily for myths of progress and success, which promise happiness through an ideology of endless *vacation*, North American Christianity has failed to attend to the deeper *vocation* of discipleship.[51]

In Hall's work, indebted particularly to Dietrich Bonhoeffer, human suffering as such is not something to be avoided but, rather, to be entered into as part and parcel of the Christian vocation. Hall deftly combines a developmental view of human growth, rooted theologically in the writings of the early Christian bishop Irenaeus, with a description of basic modes of suffering that human beings must learn to negotiate as part of what he calls the "suffering of becoming." Intended by God, such modes of suffering cannot be dismissed as suffering resultant from Adam's fall, and hence as something to be cured or fixed by the redeeming act of Christ. Instead, these modes of suffering—loneliness, anxiety, temptation, and the experience of limit—are necessary to the full experience and joy of being human. They must be entered into if we would become the kind of people God calls us to be. Attendant to that vocation of entering more deeply into life, according to Hall, is a vision of God who is not to be understood as a Supreme Being, a Father Almighty, existing beyond the world and controlling all of life. Such a God of mastery, who lurks behind and within the ideologies of the modern project, does not reflect the biblical vision of Emmanuel, the God-with-us, who is enduringly committed to the healing of the world. In the stories of Israel and of Jesus of Nazareth we discover a God who is not simply beyond us, but *for* us, and a God who *goes before* us—calling to us and forming us by attraction.[52]

Rather than "pain relief," spiritual formation acknowledges that spiritual growth is a grace-filled process, not an accomplishment, through which we grow *into* the human persons and communities God is calling us to become. These processes of receptivity and responsiveness to God, rather than *avoidance* of suffering, have compassion (suffering with) and spiritual freedom as their *telos*. Like quicksilver, spiritual freedom is impossible to possess, to hold in one's hand. The gifts of spiritual freedom— like God—are elusive. Evelyn Underhill, great teacher of spirituality, describes from what exactly we need to be freed:

We spend most of our lives conjugating three verbs: to want, to have, and to do . . . craving, clutching, and fussing . . . we are kept in perpetual unrest: forgetting that none of these verbs has any ultimate significance except so far as they are included in the fundamental verb, to *be,* and that being, not wanting, having and doing, is the essence of a spiritual life.[53]

Spiritual freedom includes being freed from what Underhill notes are the three verbs we spend our entire lives conjugating, "To want, to have, to do." Spiritual freedom, as Thomas Merton concurs, includes becoming free from: insecurities, resentments, and inordinate attachments; self-importance, self-centeredness, the delusions of the false self, underrated self, and idealized self; the captivity to a cycle of work and spend and the constant wanting of acquisitiveness, doing, and having; and the freedom from living to please others or to fulfill others' expectations. It includes becoming free from inherited myths, idolatries, and confusions.[54] Spiritual freedom frees us not only *from* things— but also *for* things. It frees us for being exactly the person we are before God. It frees us for the good and difficult work of seeking the well-being of *all.*

4. It depletes pastors' distinctive (and needful) religious authority and leadership by substituting "expert therapist" for "pastor."
The therapeutic model infects the self-understanding of the pastor—turning pastors into empathic listeners and passive sounding boards rather than spiritual guides who are "wisdom figures" in a complex, seeking world. Consequently, congregants all too often have mistakenly interpreted therapeutic listening on the part of their pastors as a welcome station for dumping complaints, finding fault with the fellow church folk, or quibbling over last week's typographical error in the bulletin rather than expressing their hunger and thirst for God or examining their own sense of desolation. If Moses thought there was murmuring in his flock, he ought to check into the current state of affairs in local congregations. Therapeutic, empathic listening has unwittingly ignited

a firestorm of complaining to the pastor instead of listening to God's activity and intentions for the congregation.

If only as a congregational pastor I had begun every conversation with a congregant in my office based on a spiritual-direction model instead of on empathic listening! The first step, of course, would always be prayer—invoking God, asking for wisdom and guidance as we sit together—and then actively listening with the congregant for God's activity in her/his life rather than receiving a laundry list of "what's wrong with the church" or "my family" or "my life" or fill-in-the-blank. Even on the occasion of valid concerns brought forth regarding love of self, neighbor, the congregation's well-being, and God's needs in the world, a spiritual director's question would be "Where is God leading in this?" rather than "What should we do about this?" More listening would be occasioned along with a broader conversation among the congregation, and an interactive model of God-Holy Spirit-congregation would be enacted.

But again, the basis of a pastor's distinctly *religious* authority to preach—rather than the authority of "pastor as expert problem solver" and "pastor as scholar"—has been eroded. Dishearteningly, a pastor's specifically *religious* authority to preach and to guide congregations remains tragically unexplored territory throughout the current mainline church.

The Distinctive Voice-Print of Preaching as Spiritual Direction

Across a nine-year span of listening to sermons—students, friends, and peers—several consistent gaps can be observed in preaching:

- an absence of historic, classic texts of spiritual wisdom;
- an absence of preaching on topics of vocation and formation;
- an absence of healthy authority and self-identity for preachers as specifically *religious* leaders; and
- an absence of information, knowledge, and skill regarding methods, models, and practices of spiritual formation that are capable of sustaining a preacher's intimate love of

God *and* vocation (and consequently the congregation's, as well!) across the span of a lifetime.

Spiritual direction as a metaphor and model for preaching begins from a much different place. Preaching as spiritual direction is not about fixing problems—life is ultimately insoluble, after all—but about ongoing guidance and orientation to God, self, others, and the world while resisting evil in all its manifestations.

- Preaching as spiritual direction does not see congregations as a group of discrete individuals in a client/patient relationship but as human persons and communities passionately needful of receiving guidance toward their individual and collective vocations, of seeking God always and in all ways.
- Preaching as spiritual direction does not surrender its gospel authority to psychological counseling models for wisdom (though grateful for the tools of psychology in group dynamics and self-actualization among churches). Instead, it mines the biblical and extracanonical resources of Christian wisdom and theology as our normative texts to be learned, preached, and lived into. As a model, spiritual direction is not unrestrainedly confident—though it is filled with ceaseless hope in God.
- Preaching as spiritual direction moves beyond understanding to a praxis of continuing commitment and development of Christian human persons and communities acknowledging the church as *paideuterion,* a school for learning.
- Preaching as spiritual direction views tragic (and ironic) suffering not as something to be avoided but as intrinsically a part of life, and as a resource for human individual becoming and communal growth.
- Preaching as spiritual direction sees its authority and self-identity in the *formation* of Christian persons and communities. It is, above all, formational in its *telos.*
- Preaching as spiritual direction relies upon pastors who understand their religious authority to be grounded by prayer, intimacy with God, and an explicit knowledge—as well as felt experience—of being the "God-person" and the spiritual guide for congregations. It is to that matter we turn to in chapter 3.

3 | Minding the Formational Gaps

Teresa of Avila suggests we consider each soul to be "like a castle made entirely out of diamond."[1] As a pastor, there were many Sundays, following a bruising week of congregational political in-fighting and plain old small-spiritedness, when my capacities to lead worship had become constricted; my spirit dampened. On such Sundays I depended completely upon Teresa's invaluable guidance. Taking my place in the pulpit, I would slowly, deliberately scan each congregant, from the left edge of the sanctuary to its outermost right edge, praying, and waiting, and watching—until each individual's soul became to me "like that of a castle made entirely from diamond." After having transformed the entire congregation into a shimmering sanctuary of diamonds with God's (and Teresa's!) help, I could with integrity lead the congregation into the presence of God, because I myself had been restored to God's presence—all due to Teresa's guidance.

The Need for Guidance

If we are fortunate, persons like Teresa of Avila have guided us toward developing attentiveness to the Divine Mystery at the heart of the universe. If we are especially fortunate, they did so during our childhood. For me, the most important guiding person was Thelma Northcutt. She often summoned her daughters to a window, "Girls! Come see! *Quick!*" to catch a fleeting glimpse of the cardinal's crimson streak across the sky or a thunderstorm's rapid approach. I raced with my sisters to the window countless times before my eyes grew able to differentiate foreground from background and successfully locate a cardinal from among all the other visual distractions. Such guidance, in discerning the foreground from the background in our lives, in glimpsing the holy in the ordinary, and learning to notice God always and *in* all ways, forms the very heartbeat of spiritual direction.

As I am writing this chapter, a thunderstorm races across the Oklahoma prairie, forsythia buds glow velvet yellow against the sky's dimming blanket; the color of quince blossoms a fuchsia alarm only God can sound. Fragrance lifts off pink phlox in candy-sweet waves. Red-headed flickers gather to peck every last ant out of the backyard, softening the ground for the earthworms and the seeds to come. The dogwoods peep tiny green promises of future buds. Dry earth aches for rain. April thunders with God's greatest commandment: *life*—and I long to call out to my Mom, "Come see! *Quick!*"

Just as my mother was to her daughters—seer, God-quickener, and guide—preaching as spiritual direction is to congregations. Such preaching functions as seer, God-quickener, guide to congregations. Consequently, *preachers* engaged in preaching as spiritual direction are to their congregations as Teresa of Avila is to preachers *themselves*: seer, God-quickener, guide. Jesus came preaching a gospel attentive to life so that we might have it more abundantly (John 10:10). Roman Catholic spiritual guide Anthony Padovano equates this attentiveness to faithfulness itself: "Life, life is what you must affirm, no matter how painfully, even unwillingly. . . . Others must know you as faithful, faithful so often that when they wonder where life lives, they will think of you as one in whom life has made a home."[2] One in whom "life has made a home" is a person who is fully attentive and awake to God. Such fully-aliveness to God (attentiveness to God's gift to us: *life*) is faithfulness.

North American Christians long for such fully-aliveness in God. They are searching for *how* to become more hospitable to God and to one another; searching for *how* to be more responsive to the vast needs of this world. Homiletician Barbara Brown Taylor astutely observes that whenever mainline Protestant churchgoers request "Bible study" they are speaking "in code," and that, actually, "'Bible' [is] a code word for God"[3] (despite the resultant Bible study's paradoxical but inevitable poor attendance!).

Though scholarship and study comprise an important aspect of our Christian becoming, we cannot develop our receptivity to the Divine Mystery at the heart of all life by self-will, self-effort, or through *ad infinitum* Bible study classes. And although the ever-bright Bethlehem star guided the journey of the Magi, it is highly unlikely such a star will guide *us* to the crèche of God incarnate. Neither the Pelagian model of *willing* one's self to becoming a deeper, better human person nor the Horatio Alger model of *improving* one's self, nor even a psychological model of *understanding* one's self fully, result in assuaging the day-to-day human desire for God yet not knowing well enough *how* to seek God.

In order to "learn God" and cultivate intimacy with God, human persons need guidance and a *guide*. The need for guidance is the reason Christian spiritual teachers have, for centuries, nurtured and cultivated practices of spiritual direction and formation. In my model of preaching as spiritual direction, the pastor, as an integral aspect of preaching, serves as *guide*—informed by twenty centuries of Christian wisdom traditions, guided, in turn, by the Holy Spirit. Preaching as spiritual direction understands the preacher as speaking *about* God while simultaneously inviting the congregation *into* the presence of God.

An ethos of preaching as spiritual direction necessitates the retrieval and reappropriation of three classic understandings from the tradition of Christian spirituality: (1) the religious authority of the preacher as God-person and spiritual guide; (2) models of authenticity and authority as found, for instance, in the Desert Fathers and Mothers; and (3) the gathered community of God as a place where people learn (specifically where they learn God): a Christian *paideuterion*.

The Religious Authority of the God-Person

The proposal I offer here reclaims a model of authority appropriate to Christian ministry: that of a theologically knowledgeable individual, well practiced in the art of spiritual formation and disciplines, devoted to the work of guiding both Christians and

Christian communities in their vocation of practicing the presence of God and relieving the suffering of God's world. The *religious* authority of such leaders rests not in their moral perfection, or in superior intellectual capacities, or in a spotlessly virtuous character (though moral well-being, scholarship, and virtuousness are certainly to be desired) but, rather, in their intimacy with God and their unquenchable desire for God's intentions toward the world to become realized.

Such a model of *religious* authority was revealed to me quite transparently by my colleague Nancy Pittman, a Disciple of Christ minister who exercised a "preferential option" for the children and infants in her church. Her office door was always open to them. Every Sunday morning, before Sunday school, a steady stream of children (from toddlers through fifth grade) made their way *inside* her office for a personal greeting. One Sunday Nancy was ill and her office door remained locked. Having never seen Nancy's door closed, much less locked, the children formed a perplexed gathering outside her office, and when finally their lingering began to attract attention, one of our church elders explained to them, "Pastor Nancy is sick. She won't be here today." Without skipping a beat (I am told), a baffled, slightly anxious four-year-old girl demanded to know, "But who will be the God-person for us today?"

The authority granted to Nancy as "God-person" by those toddlers and youngsters in 1996 differs dramatically from the notion of authority held by the influential homiletician John Wilkins in 1646, who understood the preacher's authority "as God's ambassador on earth," consequently exhorting preachers to threaten congregants "with God's wrath if they don't pay attention."[4] Models of authority subsequent to that of Wilkins, such as represented within the later homiletic of Phelps and Broadus, presumed a pastor's superior moral character in combination with a physically vigorous "manliness" that would compel those in their charge "to become better Christians."[5] Influential preacher Phillips Brooks (1835–1893) refined this latter model of pastoral authority in his Yale lectures of 1877,[6] shifting the emphasis of the pastor's authority from the preacher's physical vigor to that of the preacher's *character.*[7] In fact, priests and ministers have traditionally been called to be "Christ-like" and to model the virtues of Christ in the world. Even in the relatively less hierarchical world of Protestant-ism, ministers were expected to model Christ's virtues and author-ity in the community. As Christ was the head of the body, so the pastor was seen as the head of the congregation. Within more theologically liberal congregations, such as those within The Christian Church (Disciples of Christ), the priority of the elders over the pastor was nevertheless underscored as congregations looked to their pastor's virtues and preached word as emblematic of Christ's presence. Though the authority of the priest based on hierarchical structure and sacrament of Holy Orders, such as in the Roman Catholic communion, was rejected, ordination still meant something very significant in Protestant circles.

Throughout its history, homiletic theory has insisted that the pastor's authority is inextricably linked to character, which is in fact inseparable from the preached event. The foundational inter-face of person and preaching has remained virtually uncontested through each generation of homiletics, though each generation developed the link between the preacher's character and author-ity on different grounds. But as it became increasingly evident that preachers and pastors simply are not morally superior to other Christians and that *physical* vigor is not necessarily representa-tive of spiritual integrity, the modern model of moral perfection and physical vigor wore thin. Late-twentieth-century theological emphasis on Jesus' humanity intended to balance the Christian tradition's long-term dogmatic emphasis on Jesus' divinity. Con-sequently, one found in both Catholic and Protestant circles a new stress placed on the humanity of the priest and minister. This revised, less hierarchically authoritative view of the minister, com-bined with dramatically increasing education rates and increased salary gains among laypersons relative to clergy, resulted in a decrease in pastoral authority. Coincidentally, as baby boomers left the churches, pastors—now appearing all too human, and with decreasing cultural authority at their disposal—had little place to "vest" their authority.

Later developments (such as the Vietnam War, and the femi-nist and civil rights movements) accelerated the decline and distrust of external, positional authorities. Late-modern homile-tician Fred Craddock, brilliantly, as mentioned earlier, used irony to write to (and for) a generation that had so actively rejected authority that it had taken solace in *anti-*heroes—namely, those "without" authority. Yet, according to Mountford,[8] ultimately Craddock deftly, cleverly (and, in my view, wisely for the era to which he was writing) side-stepped the need to deal with issues of pastoral authority directly.

Postmodernity brings an additional complication to the persistent homiletic struggle with authority because (as current organizational management theory notes) postmoderns approach authority and authorities differently from previous generations. For those inhabiting the postmodern landscape, authority is "granted to people, not to positions. It will not be enough, and will most likely be counterproductive, to claim authority based upon position."[9] That the children of Dr. Pittman's congregation conferred the role of "God-person" upon Pastor Nancy was a result not of her positional *role* as pastor. These children conferred *religious* authority on Nancy because of her intimacy with God, which they experienced in her hospitality toward them each Sunday morning.

In a postmodern era that grants authority to people rather than to positions, preaching as spiritual direction—and understanding the pastor as spiritual guide—dovetail beautifully into a new hermeneutic for exploring the preacher's authority. Without in any way privileging a return to mechanized standards of dogmatic authority (a move some are encouraging, unfortunately) a deep awareness of, and attention to, the long-time Christian tradition of spiritual direction can provide a pivotal "middle path" for reimagining a genuinely experiential and embodied notion of pastoral authority. Informed by the traditions and practices of spiritual direction, pastoral authority remains strongly tethered to concerns for authenticity and human experience, on the one hand, while, on the other, picking up the Christian tradition's concerns for humility and the passionate desire for God.

Postmoderns do not seek perfect moral character so much as authenticity and trustworthiness—interpreted by the children in Nancy's congregation as inherent in someone who "talks to God" and who practices hospitality (with "the least of these"). Yet, paradoxically, while categorically dismissing external, positional authority, postmoderns seek *guidance.*

The ideal postmodern religious guide can be found in the "God-person" who is familiar with paths of prayer, practices of attention, and a life given to seeking God. Such guides reveal their intimacy with God transparently, carrying it within themselves as certainly as they carry a cell phone, a laptop, or a briefcase. Whether in a hospital room, prison cell, church sanctuary, or small-group Sunday school class, the religious leader's relationship with God is palpable, inviting, transparent. Comfortable celebrating the birth of a congregant's baby, in companioning a person in the journey through the dark night of the soul, and in visiting the convicted felon, these religious leaders are equally at home in the use of scholarship and critical methods for exegeting biblical texts and with the texts and spiritual practices of Christian mystics, saints, and reformers. When Bernard of Clairvaux or Hildegard of Bingen "did" theology, they spoke openly *of* God while simultaneously inviting others into the presence of God.[10] Such is typical of preaching as spiritual direction. The preacher's intimacy with God is *transparent*.

Gabriel Marcel's statement, "I came to love God by knowing someone in whom God dwelt" (see chapter 1), is filled with christological resonance, suggesting that religious authority is found in persons who embody the invitation *to* and the call *of* God on their lives. The authority of the spiritual guide as God-person is ultimately christological, tested by the pastor's own *transparency* to the mystery of the Christ who reveals and shows us the love of God.[11] The pastor's presence is her authority, akin to those stained-glass windows attracting illiterate medieval persons to biblical stories about which Margaret Miles writes so beautifully, positing that the visible plays a pivotal role in our understanding of God throughout Christian theology.[12]

Pastors who embody *religious* authority through prayer, practices of spiritual formation, and intimacy with God, understand that they also need relevant religious role models of authenticity and authority. Such pastors are familiar with the complexities of "knowing" and that there some ways of knowing (such as contemplative consciousness) which, as spiritual director Janet Ruffing points out, are "unavailable . . . any other way."[13] The Desert Fathers and Mothers provide ideal role models in this type of "knowing" and for developing religious authority derived by personal spiritual disciplines and intimacy with God.

Reappropriating Desert Models of Authority

In the fourth and fifth centuries, countless religious visionaries hungering for God fled from the cities (and post-Constantinian Christianization) into the desert. Egypt became the center of loosely organized—though structured—communities of monks and hermits known as the Desert Fathers and Mothers, who functioned as the spiritual guides for their time (and ever since). Many "ordinary" Christians of the time traveled from cities in which they lived to the desert carrying their deepest longings and questions, seeking the counsel of the Fathers and Mothers. According to patristic scholar Benedicta Ward:

> The key phrase of the *Apothegmata* [the "sayings" source of Desert Fathers] is, 'Speak a word' . . . . This recurs again and again, and the 'word' that was sought was not a theological explanation, nor was it 'counseling', nor any kind of a dialogue in which one argued the point . . . it was a word which would give life to the disciple if it were received.[14]

Christian pilgrims visiting the desert also brought their desire for learning the "how" of the daily, life-giving patterns that these Desert Fathers and Mothers followed. Ward notes, "The essence of the spirituality of the desert is that it was not taught but caught, it was a whole way of life."[15] It is the integrity and inheritance of this whole way of life for which contemporary God-seeking Christians hunger. Pastors of the current God-seeking era need to find ways to embody such an "essence" of intimacy with God and the life of the interior soul, that this "essence," too, can be "caught."

In their turning away from the social institutions to which they referred as "the world" and turning toward the solitude of the desert, the early monastic Abbas and Ammas gave themselves to the hard work of "striving to re-direct every aspect of body, mind, and soul to God."[16] In the post-Constantinian, post-martyrological era of the church, the Desert Fathers and Mothers modeled a new way of orienting one's life in God. With utter simplicity and material poverty they sought to love God with their whole heart, mind, soul, and strength. In the postmodern, developed world—which is all too confident that (if there is a God) God surely loves us—Christians need to be reminded that God must also be *sought*.

It is not only in the faithful activity of parenting, working, recreating, and worshiping that God is recognized but also in the *receptive* practices of *seeking* God that were so ingeniously invented by those Desert Fathers and Mothers.

Compelling in their courage and authenticity, the desert-dwelling seekers of the fourth and fifth centuries talked constantly about prayer—but not as an activity or as a form of liturgy or verbal discourse. Prayer was their *life*, a constant, moment-by-moment turning toward God. The Desert Fathers had little to say about prayer specifically, because for them "the life geared toward God was the prayer."[17] Their lives became a sign, not only for the genuineness of their search for God, but also for the self-knowledge, spiritual freedom, and thirst for a more humane society that often results from such a quest. They gained, as Ward puts it, a "personal integrity before God, without any disguises of pretentions . . . [this] is the essence of the spirituality of the desert. . . . Radical simplicity and integrity their aim and purpose."[18]

The lives of today's pastors and preachers, like those of the Desert Fathers and Mothers, are also, I believe, to be a sign, of genuine seeking of God. Self-knowledge, spiritual freedom, and a thirst for God's *shalom* are qualities sought by postmodern Christians in their pastors, just as it was sought in the era of the Desert Fathers and Mothers. Such self-knowledge and *shalom* were nurtured in the silence of the desert. An appreciation of silence and its companion, solitude, have remained constant in monastic development across the ages. Mother Teresa, herself a late-modern "product" of monastic formation, for instance, notes:

> God is the friend of silence. See how nature, the trees, the flowers, the grass grow in deep silence. See how the stars, the moon, and the sun move in silence. The more we receive in our silent prayer, the more we can give in our active life. . . . Jesus is waiting for us in the silence. It is there that he speaks to our souls.[19]

The Desert Father and Mothers encouraged (and embodied) two further virtues of which our postmodern, hurry-sick culture is in dire need: stability and patience. Amma Syncletica, for example, counseled men and women in the desert to consider prayer to be like that of a mother bird sitting on the eggs in her nest.[20] There are moments—hours, perhaps even days, weeks, and months—in prayer (and meditation) when no measurable progress can be noted. The temptation to abandon the nest—and the almost tyrannical need of the eggs for patience, attention, and presence—are emptying, wearing. The spiritual life, too, Amma Syncletica notes, is sometimes monotonous and boring. The ancient Ammas "knew that when boredom threatened, it could very well be the outward and visible sign of God's secret, hidden, inner work within the human heart and soul."[21]

Finally, in the stillness and the constant seeking of God in prayer, Desert Fathers and Mothers sought self-knowledge, to face even the painful aspects their own failings. Though, as William Harmless points out, they chose against the "active" manifestations of Christian life such as "peacemaking or healing or any of the thousand other ways of being a Christian that were possible in their time. . . . The message they offered their world—and perhaps, ours—was that to learn about stillness and prayer meant seeing harder and humbler things first, like one's true face, and one's failings."[22]

The pastor who takes Desert Fathers and Mothers as role models relies on a relational, theological authority based on intimacy with God, transparency to Christ, and devotion to prayer (rather than on external, authoritative models). Lest my proscriptive "devotion to prayer" be confused with pietistic romanticism, a cautionary word from an expert in prayer regarding this matter is in order. Teresa of Avila (it would be difficult to find anyone more devoted to prayer than Teresa) confesses to her readers, "Very often I was more occupied in wishing my hour for prayer were over, and in listening whenever the clock struck, than in thinking of things that were good. . . . and whenever I entered the oratory I used to feel so depressed that I had to summon up all my courage to make myself pray at all."[23]

While acknowledging that none of us can be experts in the world of the spiritual life (to which the Desert Fathers and Mothers, too, spent a great deal of time testifying), pastors and preachers can, nonetheless, become devoted seekers of God and guides along the way. Unlike modern Christians seeking practical knowledge to solve problems, the Abbas and Ammas viewed life more as a mystery rather than as a problem to be solved. Although they spoke of knowledge of God and self-knowledge, they meant something different from our modern understanding of knowledge as "reason" or objective facts. Rather, they meant an experiential and relational knowledge, at once honest and intimate.

The depth and authentic wrestling toward God of the desert dwellers grounded their authority. They battled their own false selves—their pretensions, their self-centeredness, their will-to-power. Through incredible patience they became free from their own inordinate attachments to things like possessions, their own sense of achievement, their control over others, selfishness, and bodily desires. God's gifts to these Fathers and Mothers—of insight, depth, wisdom, and loving compassion—make them amazingly apt models for today's pastors.

The vocation of today's pastor and preacher is to dwell among God's people—certainly not to flee from them to the desert. Yet, the fact remains that early Christians literally fled to the desert because they were drawn, attracted by the transparent integrity of the lives of the Desert Mothers and Fathers. Such a "desert" model of attraction is still valid for the wilderness of our lives and our overly filled calendars and preaching commitments. The patterns, habits, paths, and wisdom of the desert can still be used as guides for us as today's preachers, even as we guide churches and congregants.

Self-Knowledge

In *The Interior Castle*, Teresa of Avila writes insightfully to her sisters: "Knowing ourselves is something so important that I wouldn't want any relaxation ever in this regard. . . . I'll tell you . . . self knowledge is the most important thing for us."[24] Self-knowledge resides as the very heartbeat of preaching as spiritual direction. And quite unexpectedly, the pastor's complete confidence in God's unconditional love is the beginning of self-knowledge.

As Jesuit priest Peter van Breemen observes: "[God's] love [for me] is . . . the most basic and secure fact in my life. I simply let myself be loved by God. This is not so much an activity of mine but a passivity in which I let God's love soak in and permeate my whole being."[25] All too often our existential awareness of

God's love lags far behind the *symbolic* fact of our baptism, for both ordained and lay. Martin Luther instructed that we "remember our baptism"[26] in part so that we daily remember God's profound love for us. Jesus, too, struggled to grasp his God-belovedness—immediately after his baptism as "Beloved child," Jesus faced the wilderness (Mark 1:11) where spiritual director Wendy Wright speculates the temptations he faced were primarily those of discovering what "kept him . . . from really embracing the truth" that he was beloved by God.[27]

Any failure of self-knowledge on the pastor's part weakens preaching as spiritual direction. Pastors, for example, who are driven by a need for self-approval and self-affirmation unwittingly distort preaching through their own neediness. Other pastors set up conflict and strife through so-called "prophetic sermons" nurtured by pastors' neediness for conflict (rather than affirmation or love). Quite paradoxically, self-knowledge depends upon our ability to risk discovering in ourselves, in our families, congregations, and denominational structures, and in our heroes and heroines, motivations, behaviors, and realities we do not wish to acknowledge or to see. The confidence that we are loved unconditionally by God is that which enables us to risk the important work of disillusionment. Our willingness to lose our illusions in order to find ourselves and God is aptly captured by Augustine: *Noverim me, noverim te,* that is, "Let me know myself, let me know you."[28]

Thomas Merton writes that self-knowledge calls attention to the false self which, says Merton, is a form of self-delusion. Many of our dearest convictions about ourselves are simply shallow, inadequate, and wrong. One manifestation of the false self, for example, presents a highly idealized notion of one's self, *what* one does, *how* one is perceived, and *why* one does what one does. Often even "beneficent" acts of generosity, such as gift giving and hospitality or magnanimous kindness toward others, can be manifestations of a false self, masking hidden motivations such as neediness or approval seeking. A second aspect of the false self can be driven by what we *imagine* others want us to be and to become. Preachers motivated by a need for approval or by what they *imagine* others want them to be will find it practically difficult to approach preaching as spiritual direction, not having the prerequisite spiritual freedom to preach as the congregation needs rather than as the pastors' false selves demand. And finally there is the false self of underrated, doormat-like behaviors. This false self takes on tasks and projects in order to please others, instead of having a vocational *call* to the labor itself and often suffers from a great sense of indignation and of never feeling adequately appreciated.

Not only preachers, but also saints are vulnerable to the manipulations of the false self, including Teresa of Avila who confessed:

> I delight in being thought well of. So I became particular in everything I did and I thought of all of this as a virtue because I knew how to get pleasure for myself out of everything I did; all the while I neglected what was really good. . . . I myself was vain and liked to be well thought of in the things esteemed by the world. My intentions were good but my actions were wrong I became meticulous in religious solemnity and began to observe it with more vanity than spirituality.[29]

The false self that "delights in being thought well of" is capable of becoming vain even in "religious solemnity." Ironically, we must be filled with self-knowledge in order to do, as Brian Mahan suggests, the hard work of "forgetting ourselves on purpose."[30] Pastors, like all human persons, and congregations, too, suffer various manifestations of the false selves, but both pastors *and* congregations can become self-aware, self-engaged, self-reflective. Barbara Brown Taylor notes, "romance is how life gets us where life needs us to be. And by extension the romance of ordination is how God tricks us into servanthood."[31] Then wryly and poignantly Taylor sums up the quite necessary yet painful *disillusionment* awaiting pastors who have been "romanced":

> We think we are volunteering for a life of holy order, which of course turns out to the nothing but washing feet—a whole parade of them, in every shape and size, along with wet towels, muddy water, and a chronic shortage of soap. It is exactly

what God told us it would be—no more, no less—but somehow we forgot. We were thinking of leather chairs, pulpits,
prayer desks, Christmas. Without the romance, we might
never have volunteered, but thank God for the romance. It
is how we get where life needs us to be.[32]

Preachers drawn to ordination by romance inevitably discover
themselves in a congregation driven by a very different set of practical matters, a congregation in need of a deromanticized, dis-
illusioned pastor, full of wisdom of God and spiritual freedom.
Self-knowledge opens each of us to the true reality of ourselves
rather than what others might construe to be our reality. The ultimate *telos* of self-knowledge, like all aspects of spiritual practices,
is freedom. Such freedom is a foundational pillar for preaching as
spiritual direction.

Spiritual Freedom

Self-knowledge was pursued by the Desert Fathers and Mothers
for the sake of spiritual freedom. Setting aside others' expectations of preachers, as well as the masks of our professional and
social roles, is the beginning of a spiritual freedom that opens
us to receptivity and responsiveness to God's love. This goal of
spiritual freedom—which cannot be achieved in this life once and
for all—cannot be overemphasized for pastors and congregations.
Thomas Merton once described it in the following way:

> One of the purposes of the . . . [spiritual] life is freedom.
> Freedom to do what you really want. And what do you really
> want? To be able to love without impediment! To be free to
> do what in the depths of your heart you really want to. To
> be free to love what is important, what is worthy of our free-
> dom as daughters and sons of God. To be free from com-
> pulsions. To be free in the realm of imagination, which is
> very important. To be free from threatening images, people
> disagreeing with you. To be free from heedlessness, to be
> attentive to reality and fully awake to what we are doing. To
> be free to be at the disposal of reality, of others, of being

overly sensitive, which is a danger in spiritual life. . . . The real question is not, "Am I happy?" but . . . "Am I free?" Am I developing the freedom God has given me to respond with my whole self?[33]

A spiritually free preacher is the cornerstone of preaching as spiritual direction. Desert Mother Amma Theodora provides a glimpse into the qualities or characteristics of a spiritually free leader:

A stranger to the desire for domination, vain-glory, and pride; one should not be able to fool him by flattery, nor blind him by gifts, nor conquer him by the stomach, nor dominate him by anger; but he should be patient, gentle and humble as far as possible; he must be tested and without partisanship, full of concern, and a lover of souls.[34]

Similarly, Gregory the Great's model of pastoral authority advises that preachers "seek not to please men" so much as God.[35] The pastoral virtues of indifference and detachment as depicted by Amma Theodora and Gregory rely upon healthy indifference and detachment. Sadly—perhaps tragically—many contemporary ministers view themselves as politicians holding congregational factions together by virtue of their own skillful negotiations, manipulations, or "conflict resolution."

It should not come as a surprise that the Christian norm for spiritual freedom is a christological one. In seeking spiritual freedom we seek to be free in the way of Jesus—fully open and responsive to God and to our world. Nor should we be surprised that the moves of self-knowledge we have traced here of (1) trusting God's profound love for us, (2) acknowledging and confronting the illusions that distract us from being our true selves, and (3) of accepting and acting on the spiritual freedom that comes to us as a gift—take up the core theological topics of Christian anthropology. That we are created in the image of God, that we are sinners, and that we are called to newness of life in Christ—these are fundamental touchstones of Christian theology.

The work of spiritual direction reminds us, especially those of us who are preachers, that theological reflection is not simply a rarefied academic discipline, but that it illumines the depths of who we are and of who we are called to be. In the end, spiritual direction insists that the "thought God" become a "present God," and that the convictions of theology take flesh.

Reforming Congregational Ethos from Problem Solving to *Paideuterion*

The difficulties and complexities involved in growing and developing spiritual freedom are many. These difficulties and complexities understandably, in turn, need many methods or practices for spiritual deepening. But that pastors and preachers seek these things is not enough. *Communities*, too, must seek to cultivate their attentiveness to God, their receptivity to God, and to *learn* God. Preaching as spiritual direction rests on the foundational interdependence between the pastor's search for self-knowledge and spiritual freedom and that of their congregation. It is a model of cooperative, mutually supportive learning within a Christian *paideuterion*.[36]

Preaching as spiritual direction not only serves to mend the religious authority gap that postmodern preachers face, it also shifts the pastor's role from that of the (modern era's) "expert problem solver" to that of God-person and wisdom guide. In this paradigm shift from problem solving to guiding, the pastor as spiritual director evokes and engages the congregation toward constant clarification of its vocation as the people of God. Preaching as a spiritual guide, therefore, underscores the pastor's public leadership role for cultivating an entire congregation's attentiveness to the life-orienting presence of God. In the wake of such preaching, congregations become communities where both seeking God and responding to the promptings of God are central, foundational practices.

The ethos of preaching as spiritual direction itself depends upon the congregation's gradual transformed understanding of itself as *paideuterion*—a school or place of education for the mysterious, complex vocation of attending to the spiritual growth of human persons and churches, and to God's hunger for *shalom*. Benedict put it this way in his *Rule*:

Therefore we intend to establish a school for the Lord's service. In drawing up its regulations, we hope to set down nothing harsh, nothing burdensome. The good of all concerned, however, may prompt us to a little strictness in order to amend faults and to safeguard love. . . . But as we progress in this way of life and in faith, we shall run on the path of God's commandments, our hearts overflowing with the inexpressible delight of love.[37]

It is important to note the *communal* aspect of formation that Benedict has in mind. Harvard professor Sarah Coakley clarifies that for Benedict it is "endurance in community living, and not through virtuosity in private prayer [that the] heart [comes to be] enlarged . . . with unspeakable sweetness of love."[38] It is the communal seeking of God that, in itself, is intrinsically *formational*, educational for both pastor and the congregation.

In a 1926 conference, Martin Buber suggested that educators who help "bring man back to his own unity will help to put him again face to face with God."[39] It is difficult to find a more resonant description of congregational spiritual direction than that of guiding congregations (and the individuals who comprise them) to a deeper receptivity for such a "face-to-face" (as Buber writes) encounter with God.[40] While *individual* practices of spiritual direction, such as silence and solitude, self-knowledge, and centering prayer, all cultivate receptivity toward God, there also are *communal* practices that support and strengthen receptivity. Reading, studying, and critically engaging classic texts of spiritual formation, for example, all comprise such communal practices.

It is a tragedy in an era of unprecedented spiritual seeking that Christian churches and pulpits across North America have been reticent to investigate (and to adapt) their own inherited texts. These unfortunately dormant texts are strong enough to bear the burdensome weight of this postmodern era, though as David Tracy suggests, classic texts retrieved from across the centuries must be reappropriated. Consider Catherine of Siena, for example. Because of her overcommitted life advising popes and administering convents, Catherine was consistently deprived of opportunities for silent prayer, meditation, and self-reflection—surely a state of being that will resonate with postmodern Christians! Catherine noted that the Lord had inspired her "to build a little oratory within her soul where she could retire mentally and enjoy holy heartfelt solitude" while going about her "outward duties."[41] What a remarkable image for our disoriented, postmodern era—that of a quiet space which is always present *within* the soul on an as-needed basis for mental relief and spiritual nourishment! The image is visually expansive and spiritually instructive, and but one sample from among the countless riches languishing virtually unknown, but readily available to be retrieved and reappropriated.

The classic texts and themes of spiritual formation, too long neglected (and too often all too quickly—and purposefully—dismissed by modern Protestants), offer valuable guidance for how to orient our lives deeply in God. These masterpieces in the art of spiritual formation (as well as their authors) provide indispensable wisdom for the formation of Christian communities and individuals, as do modern disciplines such as psychology and sociology for the human psyche. Though, clearly, psychology and sociology are useful tools along the way, particularly in regard to individual human becoming, there are no better texts for community formation, spiritual development, and care of the soul than those by Christian spiritual masters.

Another communal practice of the *paideuterion* lies in the work of educating toward discernment in a communal conversation between (1) God, (2) God's people, and (3) God's needs in the world. Discernment relies first and foremost, always and in all ways, upon a well-informed discipline in the practices of listening receptively, communally. Discernment functions, in many ways, as the *spiritual* equivalent (for congregations and communities) of the *psychological* model's foundational rubric of individual self-understanding. The active pursuit of individual understanding (with psychological tools) is not to be left behind. However, in a *paideuterion* the emphasis is placed on *communal discernment* of God's activity and possible communal responses to that activity. Bluntly put: sermons guided by spiritual direction are effective only inasmuch the congregation reconceives its *telos* to that of *paideuterion*.

Theologian Bernard Meland notes that the ultimate goal of education involves a way "of thinking that is reflective, imaginative, spiritual."[42] Such thinking alters what lies at the heart of congregational and individual motivation. Benedict reveals the same insight when, after a thorough description of the twelve steps of humility and their fruit, perfect love of God, he notes, "Through this [God's perfect love], all he [the monk] once performed with dread, he will now begin to observe without effort, as though naturally, from habit, no longer out of fear of hell, but out of love for Christ, good habit, and delight in virtue."[43] Through such practices of reflective, imaginative, spiritual ways of thinking rather than reactive ("but we've always done it that way") or problem-solving ways of thinking, the congregation's ethos and theological underpinnings become transformed. Former motivations are gradually replaced by the insuppressible energy of God's love— palpable in times of communal desolation as well as in times of forward momentum and consolation.[44]

Given the christological norm discussed in chapter 1, Christian responsiveness must always involve discernment, learning to see with teachers like Martin Luther that God's presence, paradoxically, is hidden in our social and cultural worlds. Discerning congregations grow a capacity to grapple with and respond to insoluble issues when God's justice with mercy is at stake—for example, in situations of inherent racism and sexism. Imaginative, reflective thinking allows congregations to reframe their modern inclinations to "fix" problems into responding to them. For example, since racism cannot be "fixed," few congregations tackle the issues of racism, and even fewer congregations respond to racism. However, if "fixing" racism is not the pragmatic starting point for congregational conversation—but, rather, reflective, imaginative, spiritual thinking is the starting point—then a congregation can begin to process systemic injustices and cultivate the courage as a *congregation* to resist them. Acts of resistance attempt not to solve evil so much as to expose it, respond to it, and refuse to play by its rules.

Feminist ethicist Sharon Welch writes of the difficulty of maintaining resistance movements against intransigent social problems like the nuclear-arms race, racism, or sexism. By examining stories of African American women and men in the face of racism, Welch hopes that her readers can "learn how . . . [to] join the struggle against racism and persist in . . . [the] work against other structural problems that have as little chance of being easily overcome as does racism."[45] If, by way of comparison, a congregation hopes to "fix" racism, the congregation easily loses heart when the problem is not expeditiously fixed. Feeling overwhelmed and discouraged, congregations who've tried to "fix" racism and failed—tragically withdraw from the struggle for justice.

A congregation as *paideuterion*, then, inculcates liberating practices. Theologian Peter Hodgson notes, "God teaches through the educing or leading-forth of the human spirit into the widest range of its potentialities."[46] Discerning congregations with liberating practices view their *spiritual* lives as realities to be lived rather than entities to be attained or consumed. Such congregations are no longer operating within a congregational model evoked by preaching as pastoral counseling (discussed in chapter 2) that was so effective in the late twentieth century, yet which has become detrimental to communal formation and the demands of the early twenty-first century.

A congregation as *paideuterion* sees itself as a community (and also, individual Christians) in search of vocations. Such congregations self-consciously transform the can-do-ism of solution-oriented churches into the vocation of faithfulness that resists the temptation to measure the "effectiveness" of Christian witness. Rather than a solution-to-success foundation, these congregations are oriented to response and peace with justice.

A pastor seeking to embrace preaching as spiritual direction sees herself as God-person and guide and utilizes classic themes of spiritual direction to inform and shape the preaching. It is to the classic themes of spiritual direction and their role in shaping preaching that we now turn.

4 | FORMATIONAL VOICES

No matter how many times I had preached my way through the three-year lectionary cycle of Jesus' parables and sayings—and no matter how many times I rehearsed Jesus' command: "Love one another as I have loved you!" from the pulpit—it became abundantly, painfully clear somewhere in my seventh year of ministry that we (the congregation) simply did not know how. We didn't know *how* to love one another. Further, our failure to love could not be reduced merely to "sin" nor could it be summed up (or dismissed) entirely as the "the will-to-power," as Reinhold Niebuhr helpfully noted.[1] Nor could it be "fixed" by the good and important tools of psychology. I also like to believe our failure to love was not the direct result of my first seven years of preaching!

Week after week I found myself thinking, "We need a companion guide to Jesus' sayings and parables: an instruction manual! Something like, 'How to Love One Another in Forty Days: A Guide for Dummies.'" Which is precisely what mystics, monastics, and reformers have been doing for twenty centuries (except for the forty-day guarantee): they have developed, explored, and *tested* "companion guides" to the New Testament. So what if Paul implored us to pray without ceasing? The mystics and the Desert Fathers and Mothers are the companion guides who actually teach us and show us *how*—whether it be Benedict's *Rule*, or Teresa of Avila's autobiography, or Thomas Merton's essays in *Love and Living*,[2] or Thich Nhat Hanh's writing on *Creating True Peace*.[3]

Such writings are directed specifically to the development and formation of communities.

Though Jesus is the heartbeat of Christian community, most of his parables and sayings deal with ethical, social, and justice issues. Most of his recorded words are not concerned with the community that we call "congregation," or with the institution we call "church." Jesus was concerned with purity codes that excluded, with Roman rule that oppressed, with hungry widows, orphans, and exiled strangers. However, mystics and reformers, from the first century to today, have been concerned with precisely the matter of communal, congregational formation. They are brilliant communicators and teachers of *how* to be committed, covenanted, and baptized community members. Their work fills the instructional gap between Jesus' first-century teaching and today's congregations.

Formational Guides

Preachers who view themselves as spiritual guides and, further, who understand their religious authority to be grounded in their own seeking of God *attract* congregations who seek God and, subsequently, seek guidance from their pastors. The sayings of the Desert Fathers and Mothers provide invaluable texts for congregations seeking God and provide wonderful role models for postmodern pastors. There are, moreover, themes—classic themes of spiritual direction—developed throughout the past twenty centuries of spiritual direction, available, too.

The historic themes of spiritual direction have been cultivated (as well as practiced) by countless Christians over the span of centuries, the pursuit of which leads to wisdom, itself a cornerstone of *paidia,* that is, Christian education and congregational formation. These themes are integral life-lines for the shaping of congregations into an ethos of *paideuterion* (Christian school) where, as systematic theologian Gordon Kaufman points out, God is the symbol "to which not only persons but also communities must orient themselves, if human life is to gain wholeness, meaning, salvation."[4] This conception of God as the primary orientation of communities, as well as of individuals, provides an essential foundation "for assessing our many desires and impulses, customs, and institutions, and for disciplining them into integrated and productive selves and communities."[5]

Kaufman's wisdom that God be the symbol around which congregations organize their lives provides a helpful foundation toward them becoming *paideuteria*. But a form or a *rule* is also necessary for the very assessment of the many desires and impulses (and, ultimately, the integrated, productive community) for which Kaufman calls. Congregations devoted consciously to "the way" of spiritual formation need a *form* to follow. Not a rule in the sense of something (or someone) that must be obeyed or saluted. Nor a rule in the literalistic sense of "do this" and "don't do that," but, rather, a rule as an organizing *rubric* with guidelines that, quite literally, provide guidance along the way.

Spiritual direction's themes, curriculum, and texts provide such a "rule." This chapter describes six basic themes (from among the many, many themes of spiritual direction which might have been chosen), and proposes they provide guidance for congregations seeking to become *paideuteria*. These six themes are not exhaustive of those in the twenty centuries of historic spiritual practices! But the chosen six are reliable guides for the preacher who is learning to preach as spiritual direction. They are also reliable touchstones for congregations seeking wisdom.

1. Listening "with the Ear of the Heart"

Spiritual direction is first and foremost the fine art of listening. It is dialogical listening, involving two primary voices: the Holy Spirit or God, and self or the congregation. What does the Holy Spirit do? Or how might one "identify" the Holy Spirit's activity? In classical texts of spiritual formation, typical signs of the Holy Spirit include: a sense of being comforted, challenged, or prodded; a sense of feeling compelled to speak up for others (a) within one's interior self (regarding relationships) and (b) within the world for justice. The Holy Spirit often exhibits itself through steadiness, a sense of centeredness, of equilibrium (in persons and communities). The Holy Spirit suggests, it provokes; it can give one a sense of a holy "hunch" about a person, a relationship, a situation. The Holy Spirit often expresses itself in patience— especially guiding others toward being patient within relationships and communities. Janet Ruffing notes that though the Holy Spirit "inspirits" the activity of spiritual direction, such activity cannot normally be seen in the moment. Consequently, Ruffing proposes seven characteristic *results* of the Holy Spirit's activity:

1. It gives us a new heart.
2. It gives freedom.
3. It heals and integrates.
4. It enables our prayers.
5. It enables selflessness.
6. It leads us to truth.
7. It weaves a genuine solidarity among all creatures and the world; it *cares* when something is broken and works toward healing.[6]

Listening—with the guidance of the Holy Spirit, the congregation/directee, and the pastor/director—is the wellspring of and the authority for preaching as spiritual direction. Such listening is both skill *and* art. Among the first words of Benedict's life giving, life-changing *Rule* is *ausculta*: "Listen."[7] As the *Rule* begins, Benedict presents the "vivid image of the crowded market-place and the Lord calling out very loudly, trying to arrest the attention of passers-by in the crowd—to an invitation—to anyone who will stop and listen."[8] Fifteen hundred years later, we humans remain capable of remarkable feats to distract ourselves from listening for God.

When Benedict exhorts, "Listen . . . with the ear of your heart,"[9] he captures precisely what rapt attention is—the whole body, heart, mind, soul, and strength leaning forward into God.[10] This includes "body as well as intellect and it requires love as well as cerebral assent. It also involves mindfulness, an awareness which turns listening from a cerebral activity into a cerebral response."[11] Whole-body listening is the habit and the art of spiritual direction, typically practiced one on one by director and directee, though it is understood by both director and directee that the *real* director is the Holy Spirit (to whom and for whom both director and directee are listening). Initially, such full-strength listening is exhausting. One is emptied by its demands. But in the same way that muscle tissue is built through exercise and exertion, so, too, the interior life is strengthened by exercise and the exertion of full-bodied listening.

Listening with the "ear of our heart" is also the habit and pattern of the *preacher* whose purposefulness is spiritual direction. She listens under the persistent aegis of the Holy Spirit for the heartbeat of God within self, church, and world. She knows with Benedict that, as Esther de Waal points out, "to listen closely, with every fibre of our being, at every moment of the day, is one of the most difficult things in the world, and yet it is essential if we mean to find the God whom we are seeking."[12] Such intense listening shapes not only the interior life of the preacher, it pervades every pastoral act in which the preacher engages, from sermon preparation to pastoral visitation to congregational worship and budget meetings. Listening for God in the midst of every moment is, in fact, a privileging of God. God is in the foreground, focus, and orientation of congregational life and pastoral initiative.

It is in the privileging of God always and in all ways, as Ignatius would urge us, that the ethos of congregations is altered. The foregrounding of the mystery at the heart of all life orients congregations first and foremost to God. While it may appear oddly obvious to note the importance of God as the church's foreground and its very reason for being, the conscious orientation toward God has suffered benign neglect in many congregations, with the possible exception of worship on Sunday mornings. The work of Kaufman surfaces as essential, theologically speaking, that God is the central organizing symbol for congregations. The model of pastor as listening spiritual guide subtly alters congregational expectations of their pastor from those of C.E.O., or miracle worker, or employee who provides religious services, or therapist to become that of religious leader and guide. Congregational ethos is markedly affected by the centrality of God and listening to God.

I have personally observed a congregation's transformation from death to life, from inwardness to compassion, due to the faithful devotion of one small group of pray-ers who became friends of God within a particular congregation. The practice of prayer transformed them and slowly but surely transformed those with whom they made contact in the congregation. The church's ethos was changed, not by unanimous congregational participation in prayer, but by the attentiveness and listening skills of a small group of pray-ers who were shaped daily by the curriculum of spiritual direction, such as *lectio divina*, solitude, silence, petitionary and intercessory prayer, and journaling—and who daily foregrounded God's intentions and purposefulness in their own lives, and ultimately, the congregation's life as well.

When even a small number of congregants listen purposefully with the "ear of the heart," congregational life blooms. Classic questions of spiritual formation ("Where might God be in this?"; "I wonder where God might be leading?") lead congregations to focus less on problem solving and answer receiving, and to focus more on God-centered questions and human activity in response. The passive role of a congregation gives way to action based on the activity of God. The word *audire*, which is Latin for "to hear," shares its roots with the Latin word for "obedience," itself derived from the verb *oboedire*. Esther de Waal notes, "Obey really means to hear and then act upon what we have heard, or in other words, to see that listening achieves its aim."[13]

2. Cultivating Attention: "Behold!"

Dialogical listening, then, comprises the first central component among the six themes of wisdom as practiced in spiritual direction. *Beholding!*—the ability to *notice* and to *attend* and to *admire*—forms the second formational theme for congregations who are on the way to becoming wisdom-seeking *paideuteria*.

Attentiveness is the direct opposite of distraction, of the attention-deficit disorder epidemic in our culture. As we humans give ourselves more and more to technologies that distract and delight, without noticing what is lost—as well as what has been gained—in adapting ourselves to those technologies, we become increasingly prone to mistake *availability* to one another (via BlackBerry, e-mail, voice mail, cell phones, texting) with being fully present and *attentive* to one another. The distance between availability (and its multitasked, careless "listening") and attentiveness is profound. Preaching as spiritual direction understands the serious task of countering our culture's love for—and addiction to—distraction in order to cultivate the congregants' (and congregation's) abilities to attend to God through beholding God's activity, God's beauty, God's creation.[14] In all fairness, it must be admitted that the human capacity for distraction is not new to the twenty-first century and its jeremiad technologies. Even in the midst of the quiet solitude of grazing sheep, God apparently needed an electrifying sight like that of a burning bush to capture Moses' attention—and Moses was most definitely not BlackBerrying out there in the desert!

Twentieth-century mystic Simone Weil provides an exceptional guide in cultivating such attentiveness. Her brilliant mind, together with her passionate heart for French factory workers and their struggle for economic liberation, evoked a conflict within Weil. Deeply torn between the work of justice and that of scholarship, Weil searched diligently for a connection between study and solidarity with those who suffer in the essay, "Reflections on the Right Use of School Studies with a View to the Love of God."[15] Weil here proposes that the intrinsically valuable object of "right scholarship" is *attention*, which is at the very heart of prayer and being with God, particularly in suffering and solidarity. She argues (and laments) that "attention is an effort, the greatest of all efforts perhaps." She regrets how few of us are capable of submitting to the arduous demands of study and its resultant "habit of attention." Weil admits that there is virtually nothing harder to grow than the capacity for attention. As a test of her own capacities, Weil attempted saying the Lord's Prayer in Greek while maintaining perfect, active attention during each word uttered. "If during the recitation my attention wanders or goes to sleep in the minutest degree, I begin again until I have once succeeded in going through it with absolutely pure attention. The effect of this is extraordinary and surprises me every time."[16]

Such attentiveness is not only the purview of brilliant minds and mystics. Spiritual directors Father Kelly Nemeck and Sister Maria Coombs, abbot and hermit respectively of the Lebh Shomea House of Prayer (mentioned in chapter 1), expand Weil's intellectual analysis of attention. Integrating heart-work into the capacity for attention, Nemeck and Coombs pursue the classical contemplative life of cultivating the capacity for "beholding" God.

Each morning at Mass (the only time of the day when silence is broken) the lectionary texts are read lovingly and deliberately as the gathered congregation practices group *lectio divina*.[17]

Following the readings, in orderly dyads, fellow retreatants whisper to each other the word God "spoke to their heart" from the readings. Finally, retreatants settle in for a luminous homily by Nemeck or Coombs. Until my annual retreats there—seventeen years ago and counting now—I was not aware that every text in the Bible could be read through the contemplative-paradigmatic lens of "Behold! God!" Such is the responsible obligation and joyous labor (and practice) of preachers who seek to kindle the love of God, to engage preaching as spiritual direction. When exegeting Scripture they engage not only the most recent scholarship and interpretive criticisms but also central themes of spiritual direction that might be hidden, found, and revealed within Scripture by those who "Behold! God!"

Each day, in the anointing silence of Lebh Shomea, unbroken except for the word and creation's hymn, pilgrim-retreatants are commanded to behold God, a God wooing us through each sight, sound, fragrance, and word. Nemeck and Coombs command us to obey God's beckonings. Doing so is imperative! The underlying emphasis is not merely "Behold!" but also: "*Pay attention*; be moved, and respond!" Such "beholding" develops our facility to notice God and to respond with "loving receptivity" to this God. We learn to pay attention. Eye, ear, nose, skin, our whole heart, mind, soul, and strength are awakened. Further—we are awakened to admire what God, the beloved, has asked us to admire—as a gift—from God to us! We North Americans are given to distraction and delight and consuming. But rarely do we stop and admire what cannot be consumed, but can only be loved, adored, worshiped. The work of admiration is a seldom-practiced spiritual discipline, and central to wisdom.

Our work as preachers and pastors within the model of spiritual direction is to enhance our congregants' capabilities to attend to beholding God's activity, God's beauty, God's creation, and not only through mind and strength. Indeed, wakeful attention to God's activity is also *embodied* through sight, sound, fragrance, and sensation. Not only are we called to attend to such gifts, but to admire them and ponder them in our hearts.

The developing of such attentiveness is not the privilege of the educated elite like Simone Weil, nor is it that of the ordained and religious such as Father Nemeck or Sister Coombs. Moments for beholding God and paying attention weave themselves into the fabric of everyday, ordinary life. Mommas bathing their babies' bodies, smooth and slippery in bathwaters of everyday baptism, know this perhaps better than anyone. Ask any mother or father. Each and every profession—whether that of attorney, teacher, cook, sanitation worker, firefighter, landscaper, or nurse—surfaces methods and moments for developing attention. Even while waiting in a queue at market, bank, or stoplight—the opportunity for attending to God visits us.[18]

This is the primary work of spiritual direction: learning attention. Becoming fully alive. Noticing God. Preaching as spiritual direction explores the art of *attending* to life in all its fleeting, chaotic, thunderously spring moments and in its faithful, plodding predictability year after year after year after year: every Sunday, every committee meeting, and every potluck supper devoted to "Behold! God!"

3. Waking Us Up

Called to dialogical listening, paying attention, and "beholding," one begins to *examine* the ways in which we (as individuals and congregations) may have fallen asleep to God's intentions. There are times in every human life when a person "falls asleep" to the deep possibilities of his or her own life.[19] Congregations can fall asleep to the deep possibilities of their lives, too. This is what has happened in the recent past of many mainline churches. We, the leaders and members of the congregations, have fallen asleep to the deep possibilities of being Christ's church.

Preaching as spiritual direction awakens us as individuals and congregations to the "full range and power" of our own human hearts. It rouses us to the self-conscious awareness that we are co-collaborators with God in our lives. Preaching as spiritual direction guides us from the "taken-for-grantedness of . . . everyday routine" to "making decisions about the very meaning of [our] lives."[20]

The report in chapter 1 of congregants' hue and cry over their day-timers and their children's soccer schedules' tyrannical claim over their lives is a report of congregants' suffering the first pangs of "waking up." For these congregants, it was as if someone else, or something else, was living their lives. They were discovering that the "taken-for-grantedness" of life, based on the cultural script handed to them (with the attendant cultural timelines of marriage, babies, retirement, achievement, and all those media images of "the good life" and the security we seek), has the equivalent depth of tissue paper. Scratch the surface and one sees how superficial the cultural—and sometimes even the institutional religious—script is. It is simply incapable of bearing the weight of our lives, our sufferings, and our loves.

Preaching as spiritual direction wakes us up to the conscious awareness that our human lives (and the life of congregations) are not in fact scripted but rather a complex, collaborative process in which we are free to write our lives with God's help. When we understand this, our lives, as Merton says, then become "spontaneous, free-wheeling" and "fully alive."[21]

Understanding that we are co-authors of our lives with God's help, not only as individuals but also as congregations, means we become consciously aware that this is *our* life to engage fully and collaboratively with God. The moment we recognize this, a virtually inexpressible joy and a harrowing sense of responsibility emerge.

Consequently, congregations and individuals glimpse, as Walter Brueggemann writes, that their "purpose for being in the world is related to the purposes of God."[22] A threshold has been crossed guiding us ever deeper as we begin to explore *how* our purpose for being in the world is related to the purposes of God.

Thomas Merton exhorts spiritual directors to immediately engage the depths of their directees, advising directors to ask people what they believe they are living *for* and then to ask "in detail" what precludes their living fully for *that*. Preaching as spiritual direction, therefore, seeks to meet what Ron Heifetz calls the moral test of leadership: helping communities to face hard questions.[23] Preaching as spiritual direction awakens congregations to examine, first, any illusions into which they, sleepingly, may have fallen. Second, preaching as spiritual direction awakens congregations to consider the vocation (currently perhaps, in "snooze mode") that God might be working to "fully awaken." This process of awakening involves what Thomas Aquinas spoke of in his discussion of grace. The movement of grace always involves a *terminus a quo,* a point from which we are currently living (call it "sleep") to a *terminus ad quem*—that goal toward which we are brought.[24] It is to be hoped that preachers demonstrate by the example of their prayers and life what the movement of grace and "living fully for God" look like.

The "waking us up" aspect of preaching as spiritual direction is a vital link in the move from the model of preaching as counseling or empathic problem solving to preaching as *process*: the process of seeking God in all things.

Cognitive psychologist Robert Kegan argues that the mental demands of postmodernity create a life curriculum at which most Americans will fail. He argues that we need a "qualitatively different order of consciousness" to deal with the demands of postmodern life. That different order of consciousness relies on understanding the differences between training and education. Kegan writes, "Training increases the fund of knowledge, education (by contrast) leads us out or liberates us from one construction of organization of our mind in favor of a larger one."[25] We need *education* if we are to reach a qualitatively different order of consciousness. Much of what Protestants posit as spiritual formation (Bible study and Sunday school) relies on a *training* model of knowledge. Spiritual education, by contrast, involves giving ourselves to reconstruction: body, heart, mind, soul, and strength. This is the knowledge imparted by the classical spiritual curriculum. It provides methods and practices that in turn *wake us up* and *form* our consciousness.

4. Attending to Vocational Formation

"Waking up" and "paying attention" create new awareness in congregations and the people who comprise them. As we release the default mode of giving authority over our lives to cultural timelines and scripts, we become restless for vocational guidance. The question, "To what shall I devote my life?" emerges, and it does so with a sense of urgency in congregations and the individuals within them.

For me, the sense of vocation began one morning at nine years of age. It was Saturday: springtime. Mom had us up before 7:00 A.M.—cleaning house. Dad was running the vacuum, and my two sisters and I were in charge of dusting, emptying trashcans, stripping the beds, cleaning our rooms, shining mirrors.

I was just about to escape into freedom, having checked off the list of household chores written under my name that morning—when Mom hollered from the other end of the house, "Kay Lynn, quick! Run the compost out to the compost pile."

My mom was the queen of compost *way* before composting was cool. She collected kitchen scraps all week in a stainless steel mixing bowl—old potato peelings, eggshells, coffee and tea grounds. It was a stinky, slimy mess, and it had to be carried across three acres—to the very back of our property—where one would dump the contents of the compost bowl onto the compost heap.

As I walked past my mother on my way out the back door— the bowl of rotting scraps under my nose—I told Mom that it might interest her to know that "My best friend Audrey Barnum and her three brothers are (this *very* minute) watching *The Monkees* on T.V. and eating Sugar Pops by the handfuls (right out of the cereal box), which is what *normal* kids do on Saturday mornings." I then found the temerity to add, "I didn't *ask* to be born into *this* family."

Never at a loss for words Mom shot back: "That's right. You didn't ask to be here. God and I invited you here to make the world a better place—which requires hard work—so get going to that compost pile!"

As noted already, Walter Brueggemann says vocation is begun in those moments when we "find a purpose for being in the world that is related to the purposes of God."[26] That is what began to develop in me—the instant my mom told me she and God had invited me to be here—to meet the world's needs.

As certainly as the tides pull the ocean, there surfaces within each of us an elusive, unyielding pull toward God, toward vocational consciousness, and to the needs of the world. When we ask to what we shall devote our life, the vocational conversation includes not only occupation, but also whom and how and why we love. This aspect of vocation involves both individual or private lives as well as our congregational and public selves.[27] Since "the vocation of every human person is to live in a covenant relationship of intimacy with God,"[28] the purpose of preaching as spiritual direction includes encouraging, enlightening, and nourishing that relationship. Carolyn Gratton goes further, however, providing more pragmatic guidance in this matter of vocation. She suggests there are four primary vocational drives that continually resurface in human persons, and that typically each of us is drawn more strongly to one (of the following four):

1. A passion to help people get what they need and have a right to as human persons. Such persons become human-rights advocates, attorneys, politicians, Peace Corp workers, missionaries. They fight (legally, systematically) for those who cannot demand what they have a right to as human persons.
2. A deep response to beauty, how beauty speaks to the human soul and refines it. These people become artists, contemplatives, musicians, poets, writers, dancers.
3. A desire to uncover the truth of things for everyone's sake. Truth draws these persons like a magnet and they become scholars and teachers.
4. Goodness and kindness as the face of God. Such persons become pastors, Sunday school teachers, public school teachers, nurses, physicians.[29]

The preacher as spiritual director is acutely aware that the congregation, too, not only individuals, is a people in search of vocation. Seeking that foundational intimacy with God which is every human's vocation—and congregations' too!—means that in some sense each of us is in perpetual habitation of Mount Nebo. We are always peering across the border into the promised land, with something always remaining to be revealed.

Most certainly, this is true of congregations in the midst of vocational discernment. Preaching as spiritual direction acknowledges that there are ambiguities and hazards throughout vocational decision making, such as becoming trapped by an ill-advised or little-considered covenant (whether professional, personal, or religious). Merton goes on to propose a *telos* of sorts for vocational sorting. According to Merton, our vocational purpose is ultimately that of "learning to live . . . spontaneous, freewheeling . . . at home with oneself . . . learning who one is, and learning what one has to offer to the . . . world and then learning how to make that offering valid."[30] Preaching as spiritual direction relies on such insight into the process of human becoming. Sermons include vocational subject matter such as authenticity, self-knowledge, and the fundamental orientation of our human freedom.

Though all preaching is scripturally based, when the preacher brings spiritual direction as a metaphor and hermeneutic for preaching, topics of spiritual direction are discovered woven throughout Scripture. Parables of Jesus virtually shout: "Pay attention! Wake up! Behold!" The Gospels are downright repetitive in their imprecation: "Be not afraid but *free!*" Hebrew Scripture is overflowing with narratives of self-knowledge and the searching for and eventual finding of vocations. The work of biblical scholarship reveals—both for the good and ill of it—that we as interpreters find different themes depending upon the hermeneutic we bring to Scripture. Preachers who bring a hermeneutic of preaching as spiritual direction will find central themes of spiritual formation and guidance previously unnoticed in modern New Testament criticism and interpretation. Sermons become occasions that not only orient us to God and to biblical stories of God's activity, but also to the curriculum, methods, and texts of spiritual formation—like finding and nurturing one's vocation.

God may be calling some congregations to an altogether different vocation than the one they are currently living out—vocations based on others' expectations or false self-images. God may be calling many congregations to a much larger vocation than they currently inhabit—or perhaps, in a congregational time of famine, a smaller vocation than initially imagined. Apart from intentional, specific vocational discernment, such reimagining of congregational vocation is impossible. There is a congregation in Kentucky, actively dying, whose membership numbers only seventeen living persons, all of whom are geriatric and severely limited in economic and physiological strength. Following a discernment process with their pastor, this congregation understood that what it had—and virtually no other congregation has—is time on its hands. They discerned God calling them toward becoming a house of prayer, the model for which Merton proposed in his lecture for Our Lady of the Redwoods Monastery immediately prior to his tragically premature death.

Preaching as spiritual direction has a constant eye on exactly how—in the preached event—vocation might be caught, taught, and mentored into being. Christian vocation is defined not only in terms of our inner life but also in terms of "our response to the entire field of that life."[31] In this way we are consistently guided beyond the interface of our own personal vocational discernment and to the needs of the world. We begin to glimpse how God might see the world, each of our gifts, and how our gifts might meet the world's need.

It is worth noting that, though each of us will discover individual passions and gifts and vocations, our call ultimately from God—is *to* God. To be with God. To lead with God. To "birth" God into the future. To love God.

5. Guiding toward Sacramental Life

Preaching as spiritual direction understands all life sacramentally, "shimmering like shook foil" from sun up to sun down, comprehending each heartbeat of ordinary human experience in light of Augustine's sacramental formulation *visibile verbum* (visible word), through which God becomes known to us.[32] By way of contrast, however, preaching as spiritual direction emphasizes the human response to God's visible word through learning God, practicing receptivity toward God, and learning to receive life sacramentally. This broadening of a sacramental understanding of all life builds upon Jerome's comment regarding the Bible, "Every word contains a sacrament; there are as many mysteries as there are words," extending it to all *life*.[33] All of life is God's gift to us—and through all of life God comes to us.

John Calvin insisted that preaching, like the sacraments, is the regular and ordinary means by which God communicates the benefit of Christ's work among us. Further, Calvin claims, as church historian Dawn DeVries points out, that "like the sacraments, preaching works in appealing to the entire person (not just the intellect) through an attractive picture."[34] Spiritual direction seeks the seamless integration of word and *life* as sacrament in each human person and congregation. Preaching as spiritual direction presumes that formation by attraction is central to the work of preaching: that such preaching is "appealing to the entire person," as Calvin noted.

"Tending the holy" is an apt description of such sacramental learning of God. German Dominican mystic Meister Eckhart, for instance, advised us to be less anxious "with all that we have to do" and instead "to make holy what we do."[35] Eckhart did not mean "holy" in the sense of being set apart or of purity codes but as sacramental living. To "make holy what we do" makes everything we do sacramental—God-filled. When, as pastors, we are poring over an exegetical outline, or finding a way to introduce Douglas John Hall's theology into our church's life, or holding the hand of a six-year-old boy with cancer—each activity *is* sacrament; all sacramental, all a means of God's grace.

Preaching as spiritual direction understands *all* activity—vocational and avocational—as holy, whether one is a preacher or attorney or mom or sales manager. We find God always, in all ways. The most pedestrian moments of life can, with conscious attentiveness to sacramentality, become avenues of God's grace. Benedict, for example, in his very brief *Rule*, mentions *how* one should care for the monastery's kitchen utensils: "He [the cellarer] will regard all utensils and goods of the monastery as sacred vessels of the altar, aware that nothing is to be neglected."[36] In a *Rule* that has come to inform, influence, and guide over fifteen centuries of monasticism and church life, Benedict took care to remind us that it is in the attention we pay to the least things that we cultivate our ability to attend to the great God.

That is prayer. It is the devotion of absolute attention. It begins in us where we are.[37] As James Carroll writes, "Prayer begins with the lives we lead. . . . I presume that, since the Spirit lives in me already, I am already prone to pray."[38] Such rapt attention, and the resultant sacramental understanding of all life, is fueled by desire; it receives the breath of life from love. Teresa of Avila writes in her autobiography that true prayer consists simply "when the soul loves, in offering up its burden."[39]

And so we pray: offering up the burden of our love as we bathe our babies' bodies, smooth and slippery in bathwaters of everyday baptism then scramble into the minivan, listening to our children, driving them to school on our way to work. Our lives become sacrament whenever we bring the full force of our attention: as we work to save a family farm, as we make love to spouses and life partners, as we cook, garden, or pursue graduate studies or finish a GED, as we persist in our recovery from alcohol and drug addictions, as we practice law or answer phones, when we work for our neighborhood to be free of violence, when we resist sexism, violence, or the will-to-power in our homes and our churches and our institutional relationships—we make a sacrament of the ordinary. All of it: holy.

A sacramental understanding of all life requires that we acknowledge "the God who speaks to us in our experiences at every moment."[40] Teresa of Avila concurs: "Granting that we are always in the presence of God it seems to me those who pray are in God's presence in a very different sense, for they as it were see that God is looking upon them, while others may be for days together without once recollecting that God sees them."[41]

A sacramental understanding of all life understands the importance of living consciously in the presence of God, where we begin to see the holy in the ordinary mess of our lives. Teresa advised that we should "walk with special care and attention," especially in the faithful "performance of ordinary tasks."[42] Julian of Norwich, a giant in the world of prayer, reassures us that even in the most ordinary of bodily function, God is present. Born in 1342, this wise anchorite and mystic writes, "Food is shut in within our bodies as in a very beautiful purse. When necessity calls, the purse opens then shuts again, in the most fitting way. And it is God who does this."[43] Julian's wisdom that nothing lies outside the presence of God, suggests that a fitting response to this mysterious presence is a sacramental understanding of *all* life.

Buddhists such as Thich Nhat Hanh refer to such attentiveness as "mindfulness," As Hanh notes, mindfulness can be practiced "when you walk, stand, lie down, sit, and work, while washing your hands, washing the dishes, sweeping the floor, drinking tea, talking to friends, or whatever you are doing. . . . Each act must be carried out in mindfulness."[44] Preaching as spiritual direction acknowledges that the work each one of us gives our daily lives to is holy, as is the congregational work to which we give ourselves, too. Sermons, then, are sacramental themselves, calling us to recognize the sacred in each breath and to live and work in moment-to-moment recognition of God's presence to us, and God's presence in the world *through* us.

When God seeks to change human history, God enters into history through the risk of birth, through human beings, sacramentalizing humanity. Social philosopher Hannah Arendt noted that every child represents the birth of the new, of *natality*: "The new beginning inherent in birth can make itself felt in the world only because the newcomer possesses the capacity of beginning something anew."[45] Each child enacts something utterly unique, utterly *new* in the universe, the new, the hopeful release us from present oppressions. God enters in to history through the natality of individual children, adult lives, and through congregations. Such is a sacramental understanding of all life.

Theologian Douglas John Hall uses the analogy of a musical score to explain how God works in the world. God changes the world like a composer adding a new voice to an orchestral score. Add a new voice? It changes *everything*.[46] The preacher who understands her or his vocation as spiritual director seeks daily to become a *voice* through which God speaks with individuals and congregations—to change the course of events in the lives of human persons and subsequently in the world. Even the preacher's voice, then, is sacramental, becoming a "visible word" through which God works.

6. Seeking to See as God Sees

As the director and directee begin to imagine together—with the Spirit's help—how God sees, they begin to glimpse beyond human desires all the way to *God's* desires. People and suffering and beauty and anguish and earth and delight are experienced in depths and heights previously missed. Life takes on unimaginable dimension and purposefulness. While previously we may have *known* God's unconditional love, we begin to *believe* it and to live out of it. Preaching as spiritual direction guides the congregation (as with director and directee) to see as God sees. Analogically speaking, just as the director who listens to the directee then offers insights, reframes questions, and sometimes lovingly challenging the directee—so, too, does the pastor with the congregation.

Within the congregation's preoccupation with how God sees, compassion begins to emerge. Self-compassion even sallies forth so that loving neighbor as self becomes a dynamic possibility powerfully fueled by a healthy, God-centered self-love. Selfishness finds itself able to step aside, and a hunger for life more abundant bursts forth—not only for one's self or for one's own children. Great battler for social justice Dorothy Day said it best when she confessed, "I wanted life and I wanted it abundantly. I wanted it for others, too."[47] When congregations begin to glimpse how God sees, they find themselves harboring life more abundant for everything that has life and breath, and even for earth's soil.

When "glimpsing God," justice and mercy begin to preoccupy us as congregations and the individuals that comprise them—so that even our proprietary self-concern for protecting and ensuring that our own nuclear family and our own congregation remain safe begins to collapse as we contrast such self-involved desires with God's desire for life more abundant for all God's family: *for everyone*.

Preaching as spiritual direction, then, is not a problem-solving or fixing approach. It is a process of learning to know God's infinite love and regard for us and of seeking to see as God sees. Once again, the rich tradition of spirituality, a treasury of sorts, provides essential source material for such preaching. Scriptures, themes, and illustrative material for sermons are interpreted through the hermeneutic of attentiveness, beholding God, and seeking to see as God sees. A triune relationship is embodied between preacher, congregation, and the Holy Spirit.

Preaching as Spiritual Direction: A Biblical and Theological Hermeneutic

While paying rigorous attention to exegesis and the finest historical-critical scholarship available, pastors who bring a hermeneutic of spiritual direction to bear upon their preaching will find within scriptural texts a rich array of images, characters, conflicts, and themes fruitful for the formation and guidance of both persons and congregations. Viewed from the perspective of spiritual direction, the sermon becomes an occasion that not only orients us to God and to biblical stories of God's activity, *but also to the curriculum, methods, and practices of being formed as a people of God*. Though, as emphasized already, all preaching is scripturally based, preaching as spiritual direction will specifically utilize the six themes of spiritual direction discussed above as herme-neutical lenses. These hermeneutical lenses function as discovery points of encounter with the biblical message.

Theologian David Tracy has persuasively argued the vital importance of historical biblical criticism for both the pastoral and theological interpretation of Scripture. Tracy has also sug-gested, however, that biblical criticism and its exploration of various structural interconnections of the text within its original setting may aid—but cannot be fully adequate to—the full herme-neutical encounter between text and interpreter. Beyond histori-cal and structural analysis of the text, therefore, Tracy suggests that one must risk an engagement with the text.[48] The six themes of spiritual direction I have proposed as foundational for the preacher evoke that deeper hermeneutical encounter for which Tracy calls.

Further, the six categories provide a distinctive biblical and theological understanding of the gathered community. Affirm-ing that God is present in and through the world, preaching as spiritual direction celebrates biblical poetry and narratives as vital to the religious community's identity but also explores con-temporary experience for signs of God's presence and guidance. Preaching as spiritual direction wakes us up and alerts us to the presence of God stirring in our midst. More than awakening our consciousness in a general sense, preaching as spiritual direction moves us to behold that presence in our ordinary, moment-to-moment experience so that we might be responsive to and respon-sible for nurturing our continued attentiveness—and response to God's needs in the world and our suffering neighbors. Insofar as such preaching encourages habits of attentive beholding and responding, it also guides the vocational development of both persons and the congregation as a whole, providing the basis for the narrative of the congregation's distinctive religious journey and identity.

Because of spiritual direction's primary development within the Christian tradition, both prior to and following the Protes-tant Reformation, one might think that the practice and applica-tion of spiritual direction is strictly limited to a Roman Catholic, or at least traditionalist, theology and audience. The process of spiritual direction, however, is fully compatible with a wide range of Christian theologies—from evangelical assumptions about the reality of God to feminist, process, panentheistic, and liberationist models. Spiritual direction offers, within these models, a deeper attention to, and practice of, the presence of God at work in the world. What is important is that pastors and their communities come to some shared sense of the models of God with which will guide their common direction and shared story.

5 | Mending the Gaps

This book has emphasized two equal, interdependent parts as essential to preaching as spiritual direction, namely the spiritual life of the preacher and the *aim* of preaching itself. The book proposes that preaching's purpose be that of spiritual direction and formation.

Because preaching as spiritual direction is inextricably linked to the spiritual life of the pastor and preacher, the second part of this chapter addresses "how" a pastor's ongoing spiritual formation, interior vitality, and spiritual balance can be nurtured. Three key pairs of interdependent *methods* (from the art and practice of spiritual direction) upon which preachers can rely for their spiritual balance are explicated. These methods are relevant not only to the interior lives of pastors and preachers. They are also vitally important interpretive keys for exegeting and shaping the lives of congregations.

The Preacher

The final requirement toward my becoming a spiritual director was quite straightforward: participation in a weekend retreat. Jill, the director, announced excitedly that the retreat location had a labyrinth for us to walk. I yawned. Labyrinths inevitably evoke a mixture of boredom, dread, and consternation in me. "What on earth makes all those labyrinth fanatics tick?" I have always wondered to myself. "Why don't labyrinths tick for me?"

The retreat fell on an early April weekend and four of us (spiritual-directors-in-training) carpooled to the retreat center where, an hour later, we arrived in a burst of energy and laughter. Our retreat director eventually settled us down with several hours of *lectio divina* and meditation. Finally, at noon, it was announced that the duration of the afternoon would be spent in silence, solitude, self-reflection, and walking the labyrinth.

I decided—as with any unpleasant task—to get the labyrinth assignment out of the way immediately. I marched myself out to the labyrinth like an Army recruit reporting for duty. Earlier that day, Jill had instructed us on how to walk the labyrinth—suggesting that we walk it "like a bride," with a rhythmic, measured gait: right step, left step, step together, *hold*; right step, left step, step together, *hold*. I began the bride-like walk at the entrance to the labyrinth thinking, "This is *ridiculous.*"

As I made the first hairpin turn, my right foot came down on an overgrown lump of buffalo grass, and as I gently fell to the ground I realized this particular labyrinth was about sixty feet across, at the diameter. I did a quick guesstimate of how many bride-steps in "real" time I was looking at, and figured I would be held hostage by this labyrinthine labyrinth for approximately an hour. Picking myself up, I resumed the bride-walk muttering under my breath, "Only for Jill."

The first length of the labyrinth I faced a biting north wind and within a few minutes my eyes were streaming, my nose running, and my fingertips growing numb. I'd forgotten to bring a scarf, gloves, and a Kleenex. I hadn't noticed the sharp north wind when I'd left home earlier that day. Then? I made the next hairpin turn—which doubled back south. In an instant the warm rays of April sun were on my face, and a view of an orchard filled with budding fruit trees lay before me. I settled in with a certain joy at the beauty, the sun on my face, and the promise of spring.

But immediately, the next hairpin turn and the biting north wind returned as did the tears, streaming nose, numb fingers; the uneven clods of grass reaching for me like the creepy trees from *The Wizard of Oz.* I wanted to hurry to the next hairpin—to feel the sun on my face again, the wind at my back. I wanted to rush to the good part—to glimpse the promise of spring and that wonderful view. But life is a *balance,* and the labyrinth is a *balancing* practice.

Our spiritual lives are a constant interplay, a dynamic process. At the heart of this dynamic interplay are several interdependent pairs of seeming "opposites," such as activity/receptivity, consolation/desolation, and detachment/attachment, which are, in fact, mutually interdependent. Each of these pairs plays a dynamic role in sustaining, interpreting, and shaping the spiritual life and intimacy with God—for individuals and congregations. Spiritual direction guides one toward noticing these pairs and also toward seeking their equilibrium, that is to say, balance. Balancing practices such as walking a labyrinth help us glimpse not only the process of our lifelong journey toward God, but also the interplay and balance between these three interdependent pairs.

Preaching as spiritual direction is attentive to the constantly changing dynamic of the spiritual life in the congregation *and* the interplay between activity/receptivity, consolation/desolation, detachment/attachment. Such knowledge informs the pastor's preaching and also the pastor's hermeneutic of Scripture *and* of congregational life. Pastors who pay attention to the powerful energy of these "operative pairs" will glimpse them not only in Scripture and congregational dynamics but their preaching also will be informed by them. Such "tools" as activity/receptivity, consolation/desolation, and detachment/attachment are essential to preaching as spiritual direction, the pastor's own spiritual balance, and, consequently, the congregation's. It is to these tools we now turn.

Activity/Receptivity

Spiritual growth and formation have no quick fixes. There are no "techniques" or technologies that will—by virtue of being applied—achieve immediate spiritual growth or development in human persons or congregations. There are, however, practices that, over time, create hospitable spaces in which spiritual growth can occur. All spiritual practices can be categorized within one interdependent pair, namely *activity* and *receptivity.* Unfortunately, within all too many cultures in our contemporary society, activity and receptivity are viewed as the opposites of one another rather than interdependent spheres, each in need of the other to become whole.

Gerald May has poignantly noted, for example, that overcommitted, overactive, overscheduled North Americans are so busy fulfilling all the commitments they've made they've forgotten why they made them in the first place![1] Paradoxically, we lose—through constant activity—our connection, experientially and spiritually, to "the Divine mystery at the heart of all that is,"[2] which drew us to make those commitments: to our partners, marriages, children, and families, to our churches, and to the public good. The same claim may be made of congregations that are so busy fulfilling their program commitments they have lost touch with the Divine Mystery. Although every commitment was made with the best of intentions, constant activity disorients congregations as well as human individuals. Congregations wishing to be in relationship with God need receptivity as well as activity; that is, human persons and institutions need both receptive *and* active spiritual practices. As Parker Palmer points out, human activity and active practices of spirituality help to "shape the world," while receptivity and contemplative practices "help us see reality."[3]

Psychiatrist and spiritual director Carolyn Gratton notes that "to wake up to the range and power of [our] own human hearts"[4] is foundational to the work of spiritual development. The full range of our human hearts includes physical wellness, mental and personality wellness, relationship/outreach wellness, work/play wellness. As chapter 1 relates, my own spiritual recovery as an adult began with the realization that I was alarmingly out of shape, "physically a wreck." It was in daily aerobic classes that I began to catch my breath—literally and spiritually—as I began to wake to the full range of my human heart, physiologically and spiritually. Aerobic exercise, most certainly an activity, was the necessary balance to my overly inactive life, physically speaking. "Waking up" is an essential component toward healing the dangerous imbalance in persons and congregations between the highly overactive lives we are living and the typically severely undernourished receptive practices that may go neglected for days and weeks (or even years).

Active practices include such things as visiting the sick and imprisoned, clothing the naked, feeding the hungry, and working for justice. Also included in active practices are *congregational* activities such as worship, singing in the choir, participating in committee, board, and congregational meetings, potlucks, youth groups, prayer groups, evangelism, Sunday school programs; mission activities, social justice rallies, and fundraisers—and so many more activities than any single list can contain! Most congregations do quite well in terms of *active* practices of congregational formation; in fact, most Christians individually, too, operate quite effectively within the sphere of active spiritual practices. But, as Thomas Merton suggested, "We are perhaps too talkative, too activistic, in our conception of the Christian life. Our service of God and of the Church does not consist only in talking and doing. It can also consist in periods of silence, listening, waiting."[5]

Receptive practices include such things as *lectio divina*, meditation, vocal and mental prayer, devotional reading, solitude, *examen* (see below), retreat, silence, fasting, and contemplative prayer; labyrinth walking, gardening, prayer groups, and prayer walks. Most individuals—and certainly most congregations— seldom give themselves to the sphere of receptive spiritual practices.[6] Most receptive practices require solitude and silence. Merton suggests that most of us avoid silence and the "inner self" because we are unable to face "ourselves . . . [so] we keep running and never stop."[7]

Gratton explains that every culture not only has patterns and practices which give life and form and shape to human persons and communities but also has within it patterns and practices which "mal-form" persons and communities, spiritually speaking. Those of us raised within the nano-second, drive-through-window culture of the United States, for example, hate to *wait*— yet the Hebrew Scriptures are quite literally filled with injunctions imploring human persons to *wait* for God. The Psalms and Isaiah alone exhort human persons to practice *waiting for God* thirty-two times. U.S. culture, with its seemingly insatiable desire for more (*everything!*) and its predilection for a virtually frantic, frenetic pace, has malformed us, shaping us largely by the active paradigm, as individuals and as congregations (and sadly, as pastors). John Kenneth Galbraith describes graphically the incessant struggle to satisfy increasingly disproportionate wants, comparing the hectic pace of North Americans to that of "the efforts of the squirrel to keep abreast of the wheel that is propelled by his own efforts."[8] Juliet Schor, in her book *The Overworked American,* observes:

> Millions of working parents see their children or spouses far less than they should or would like to. Working mothers complain they have no time for themselves. Volunteer work is on the decline, presumably because people have little time for it. Employed Americans spend long hours at jobs that are adversely affecting their health—through injury, occupationally induced diseases and stress. My explanation for this paradoxical behavior is that people are operating under a powerful set of constraints: they are trapped by the cycle of work-and-spend.[9]

Overcommitment has many root causes, spiritually speaking, beyond the monetary constraints about which Schor writes. We overcommit out of a sense of duty or out of a sense of doing the "right thing," or because "something needs to be done and there's no one else to do it." Parker Palmer sums up these behaviors with the sad observation: "Too many of us spend time doing things for which we have no heartfelt reason."[10] We commit to doing something prior to discerning whether or not it is an activity to which we are, in fact, called. We say yes before considering whether such a commitment is part of God's intention for our lives and congregational life. Our very heart and soul may be aching for silence, solitude, for spending time delighting in God—and yet we are blind to this need for receptive, quiet, restorative, and balancing soul-work. Such blindness is partially the result of the malformation we receive from our culture's preferential option for activity *over* receptivity.

But in a careful reading of the Gospel accounts, we observe Jesus demonstrating a balanced pattern of active ministry alternating with receptive prayer, rest—or simply being with God. Jesus alternated between doing *for* God and being *with* God, between action toward the kin-dom and contemplation of that kin-dom, between activity toward God and receptivity *of* God. In Luke, for example, we read that Jesus, after healing a man with a withered hand (6:6-11), "went out to the mountain to pray; and . . . spent the night in prayer to God" (6:12). Likewise, Mark 1:21-35 records a very busy, exhausting day in the life and ministry of Jesus, after which Jesus retreats to pray: "In the morning, while it was still very dark, Jesus got up and went out to a deserted place, and there he prayed."

Sometimes Jesus' activity is followed by receptive prayer with "only the disciples near him." For example, following the Lukan narration of the very active miraculous "feeding of the five thousand," Jesus retreats with the disciples near (Luke 9:18a). Then, immediately following a conversation with the disciples (Luke 9:18b-27), Jesus retreats with a few close friends, "Peter and John and James, and went up on the mountain to pray" (Luke 9:28). The Gospel narratives portray a Jesus who provides a remarkably consistent example of obedience to the intrinsically valuable balance of *both* spheres of the spiritual balance between activity and receptivity.

Preachers who engage in preaching as spiritual direction are attentive in their own lives to the alternating practices of receptivity and activity as modeled by Jesus. They, too, as preachers, alternate preaching about the *activity* of Jesus with the *receptive* practices Jesus followed. Such preachers lift up moments in which Jesus practiced contemplation, enjoying God, rest, retreat, and silence—as often as they preach his active ministry of healing, teaching, and those exhausting preaching tours he made!

Congregations become aware of their need for receptive congregational practices such as group *lectio divina*[11] and contemplative prayer (for example, *Taizé*). Preachers and congregations also grow in awareness of the need to practice *receptivity* toward God individually, as Jesus did, in quiet solitude—a lonely place or a mountaintop.

Parker Palmer notes that contemplation—far from passivity—is active, in that it transforms our consciousness, our attentiveness. The deeper the contemplative work, "the more clearly [our] true work emerges . . . [and] the claim of that work on [our] lives."[12] This transformation *through* contemplative practices makes a significant impact upon the world and our families and our church—as certainly as strategic action does. It is to such receptive, contemplative practices that *sustain* our spiritual lives as pastors, congregations, and persons—and reimagine the world—to which many of us and our congregations need to return, finding balance with the activity of our lives.

Consolation/Desolation

In the midst of that seemingly endless labyrinth, I wanted consolation. But the relentlessly deliberate, slow-paced discipline of the "bride-walk," in combination with the mirroring hairpin turns (and mere distance!) of the labyrinth, kept me in perfectly equal parts of desolation *and* consolation, over and over and over and over again. I remembered Jill teaching us that desolation and consolation are not opposites but, rather, that they are part of the balancing wheel, in actuality coexisting. Life is neither consolation nor desolation—but both. Our *spiritual* lives are neither consolation nor desolation—but both. Walking a labyrinth reveals both consolation and desolation, in "compressed" time. All life is illumined by such balancing "compression."

Quite often a person's—or a congregation's—levels of consolation and/or desolation run just below the surface, "off the radar screen," where they are capable of creating a sense of moodiness or disequilibrium. Understandably, such disequilibrium affects an individual's responses to other people, situations, and to God, frequently evoking strong emotions or defensive postures. Teresa of Avila reports having received a "consolation" from God in which she was reassured that the interplay and disequilibrium between consolation and desolation are not to be feared:

> God once told me, by way of consolation, not to worry . . . and said this very lovingly . . . for in this life we could not always be in the same condition. Sometimes I should be fervent and at other times, not; sometimes I should be restless and at other times . . . I should be tranquil. But I was to hope in God and not to be afraid.[13]

Though neither consolation nor desolation are to be feared, the results of disequilibrium, gone unnoticed, are. Because not only individuals, but congregations, too, suffer from disequilibrium, learning to notice (and to interpret) consolation and desolation are key practices for preachers who engage in preaching as spiritual direction. Spiritual director Margaret Silf identifies the following among the symptoms of *desolation*, which:

- turns us in on ourselves;
- drives us downward in a spiral ever deeper into negative feelings;
- cuts us off from community;
- makes us want to give up on things that used to be important to us;
- takes over our whole consciousness and crowds out our distant vision; and
- drains us of energy.[14]

Silf's list of symptoms is relevant not only for individuals but also for mainline congregations who suffer an imbalance toward desolation and its subsequent inward focus, negative feelings, and isolation from broader communities (local, ecumenical, denominational, regional, universal). Congregations that have dwelt for too long in desolation—and having not experienced its counterpart, consolation—often lose heart. Their sense of mission and God's purposefulness in their life weakens. Such congregations suffer symptoms remarkably similar to those of depression and chronic fatigue syndrome. Desolation, however, when properly recognized and received, invites turning toward God wholeheartedly. Such a movement toward God, paradoxically and simultaneously, turns desolation's inward focus *away* from self and *toward* others—just like a labyrinth's hairpin turns.

Ignatius advises individuals against "going it alone" in desolation but, rather, reaching out and seeking companionship. For many mainline congregations this means, for example, turning away from a defensive, self-oriented stance of "survival" and entering desolation's wilderness and wisdom, by returning to God and the needs of the suffering world and, paradoxically, by doing so returning to God.

Though congregational desolation is often a sign of God's attempt to do "a new thing" and awaken the congregation toward new life, it is important to recognize that decisions (either congregational and/or individual) should never be undertaken in a time of desolation—nor should previously made decisions be altered during such a time. Ignatius advises that we remain mindful that desolation is a normal aspect of spiritual growth. Desolation is a time to place one's trust more deeply in God, however difficult. Desolation is also the time to remember and revisit previously experienced moments of *consolation*. Just as there are signs of desolation, there are signs of consolation. As summarized by Margaret Silf, *consolation*:

- directs our focus outside and beyond ourselves;
- lifts our hearts so that we can see the joys and sorrows of others;
- bonds us more closely to community;
- generates new inspiration and ideas;
- restores balance and refreshes inner vision;
- shows us where God is active in our lives and where God is leading us; and
- releases new energy.[15]

It is difficult to imagine a more of "what the church needs now" than a life-giving interplay—and conscious awareness—of desolation and consolation! That consolation is not limited to a sense of happiness, or well-being. In fact, one can experience a profound sense of consolation in the midst of very difficult circumstances. Consolation is, quite simply, a deep connectedness with God, perhaps captured best by the psalmist as God's presence *especially* in the midst of desolation, "If the LORD had not come to my help, I should soon have dwelt in the land of silence. As often as I said, 'My foot has slipped,' your love, O LORD, upheld me. When many cares fill my mind, your consolations cheer my soul" (Ps. 94:17-19).

Ignatius advises that, during times of consolation, we "savor the strength" and dwell on the attributes consolation brings. Congregations should, quite literally, *memorize* the experience of consolation so as to recall it later during times of desolation. A spiritually free person (and a spiritually free congregation) does not fear or dread desolation even in the midst of the greatest consolation and vice versa. A spiritually mature person holds lightly to both—and knows they coexist; like every Sunday morning during worship when so many of us know the desolation of suffering: cancer, war, brokenness, and despair while at the same moment others of us are joyous: hope filled, healthy, and achieving. Neither suffering and its diminishment nor joy and its accomplishment can be *fully* real without the other. Desolation informs consolation, consolation informs desolation, within the balancing rhythm of the labyrinth, in life, in congregational life, and in preaching.[16]

Preaching as spiritual direction will note moments (or seasons) of consolation and desolation within the congregation; it will also take note of the preacher's own consolation and/or desolation; it will notice themes of consolation and desolation in the exegesis of Scripture; it will be informed by all these things in the preached event.

Developing the capacity to seek God always in all ways—even in the midst of consolation, and its profound connectivity with God, and in the midst of the valley of the shadow of death and its desolation, is crucial to our spiritual development. Negotiating an inner peace or equilibrium (between consolation and desolation) is necessary for congregations and persons in order to clear a space to listen for the Holy Spirit's guidance.

The resultant quietened, balanced place is one in which creative and life-giving companionship between congregations and God, between congregations and the world, are nurtured, formed, sustained, and—in due season—challenged. Such a state of charity relies on another interdependent pair in the balance and equilibrium of spiritual formation: detachment/attachment.

Detachment/Attachment

Larry Dossey, M.D., has devoted much of his life's work to exploring the effects of prayer and healing.[17] Instead of merely measuring the effects of prayer, Dossey has sought to determine whether some prayers are more effective than others. Dossey concluded that "although science tells us *that* prayer works, it cannot tell us *how* it works."[18] But he did discover that one of the best approaches to intercessory prayer (or prayers of petition) is a form known as *nondirected* prayer, "May the best possible outcome prevail."[19]

This prayer for the "best possible outcome" is in fact itself a practice of spiritual formation known as *detachment*. The one who prays in such a manner has *detached* from praying for a specific, *directed* outcome. The one praying for the "best possible outcome" has abdicated a personal sense of "what ought to happen," moving from an "attachment" to one's own desires and purposes to a "letting go" into the purposefulness of *God's* intentions.

Practicing a healthy form of detachment is not only good for those who pray (and consequently for the recipients of those prayers) but also for congregations. Christians, preachers, and congregations who become inordinately attached to a certain, well-intended outcome—whether it be a new evangelism program, Vacation Bible School curriculum, or choosing new carpet and décor for the sanctuary—can often overlook (or neglect) *God's* intentions. Congregations, however, which are familiar with the spiritual practices of receptive listening for God and the Holy Spirit's movement as well as with the six foundational themes of spiritual direction (see chapter 4) are better able to "hold lightly" to their own inclinations, ever pressing toward where God might be leading in a specific situation. Such "holding lightly or loosely" to attachments precludes a congregation's becoming *inordinately* attached to an outcome that drives congregational behaviors. Rather, a healthy *detachment* from desired outcomes clears space for the Spirit's leading and God's purposefulness in the congregation.

Ignatius was well aware of the many dangers of inordinate attachment. Such attachment is selfish, grasping, thoughtless, and all too often motivated by a will-to-power, which Reinhold Niebuhr so accurately, *poignantly* described.[20] The consequences—of holding tightly rather than *loosely* (and subsequent congregational barreling full steam ahead)—typically include misunderstandings, hurt feelings, resentments, unfulfilled possibilities, and brokenness. Holding too tightly to one's own desires—or a congregation to its own desires—is commonly rooted in what Ignatius referred to as the uppercase Self that likes to compete and conquer for the sake of "honor, riches, and pride." The uppercase Self holds onto personal attachments with a very tight grasp. Ignatius warns that the Self will blithely manipulate situations to its own advantage, either for gaining the approval of others or to shore up its myth of self-sufficiency. Ignatius advises that we transform the uppercase Self into the lowercase self which "holds lightly" to its own predilections, consequently creating a healthy form of *indifference.*

The spiritual practice of *indifference* is not a self-calculating or cold emotional state. Rather, it may best be described as a state of "neutrality" in which one resigns personal agenda, attachments, and desires in order to listen for direction. "Indifference" implies *flexibility.* Indifference is ultimately a liberating process toward "finding God who sustains, supports, and lures toward the future in the process of life. While few people truly enjoy this degree of freedom the *desire* for it remains essential."[21] Ignatius communicated this in yet a further way when he suggested that we practice "not preferring."[22] Paradoxically, it is through *not* preferring (or indifference) that we encounter spiritual freedom.[23] Detachment is the conscious practice of not preferring—in a specific situation—for the purpose of noticing where God might be leading rather than where we would prefer to go! "Not preferring" includes freedom from self-identity in terms of either what we possess or do and also freedom from self-identity as validation from others, freeing us from whatever would restrict us, opening us to become more and more available to God.[24]

Clinging to attachment is *not* life giving, though it is as much a part of our humanness as waking, sleeping, and breathing. Gerald May notes:

> While intellectually we may recognize that attachments are fundamentally related to suffering, we cling to the conviction that at some level and to some degree they are absolutely necessary for the preservation of life. . . . We feel our worlds would fall apart if attachments ceased to drive us. All motivation would be lost. Everything we have worked for and held dear might crumble. . . . [Attachments] are the bonds that, though they restrict and enslave us, also secure our self-images in the world. . . . We will do anything to avoid having to part with them.[25]

My spiritual director describes attachments as "kidnappers of attention" that pull us away from "our fullest response to God." Attachments are, at best, spiritual detractors that can keep us in constant interior turmoil, on an emotional roller coaster.

Spiritual director Jane Vennard proposes that a spiritual director is a "compassionate observer who sees [the directee's attachments] with compassion and holds out the hope and promise of God's abiding love."[26] It is in the care of such a compassionate observer that we become able as individuals (*and* congregations) to pay attention to our attachments, to develop compassion for them, *and*, paradoxically, gain the capacity to let them go.

Pastors who understand and practice preaching as spiritual direction will necessarily inhabit the role of "compassionate observer," not only seeing clearly the imperfections and failings of congregational life, but also helping congregants "find their connection to wisdom, compassion, and the promise of God."[27] Preaching as spiritual direction involves the formational practice of detachment in which one "holds loosely" to one's desires in an effort not only to understand them but also to become more aware of the needs and desires of others. Detachment, or a *healthy* indifference to one's own will, frees the Holy Spirit to "hold sway" within our congregational decision making. Detachment is based on a self-giving generosity toward God and toward one's neighbor. It prays for the "best possible outcome," something that only God can know—but human communities can (with enough healthy detachment) come to discern, sense, and move toward.

Ignatius used the term *indifference* rather than detachment, though he warned against practicing indifference toward *persons*, emphasizing, rather, that indifference, while not valuable for its own sake, is necessary for the process of gaining spiritual freedom. Preachers who utilize indifference and detachment as spiritual practices for preaching are noticeably *free* in their preaching; free from blaming, scapegoating, resentment, anger; *free* from placating, pleasing, or seeking approval; *free* from preaching that is entertaining ("Look! Aren't I funny and *lovable!*"), coquettish ("Aren't I *cute!*), superficial ("This sermon will take only ten minutes of your time."), or manipulative. Pastors who are well equipped in practicing "neutrality" and who do not "prefer" are free to *listen* to God both in the midst of congregational business *and* worship; free to guide congregations in the midst of a sea of conflict; free to *explore* where God might be leading; free to *be* with God. In short? Free to lead as spiritual guides. The preacher who is *free* is available to risk the very real, the very depths, each time she enters the pulpit—for life itself is at stake: the life of the congregation *and* the life of the suffering world.

6 | FORMATIONAL SERMONS

THOUGH I PROVIDE HOMILIES FOR MY SEMINARY COMMUNITY'S Morning Prayer liturgies each week, I am no longer a full-time congregational preacher or pastor. Currently, I am an itinerant preacher most typically engaged on a guest basis. Here I offer a sampling of three recent sermons, preached in a variety of contexts, in which I set out to demonstrate by example what preaching as spiritual direction does.

Each of the three sermons incorporates different facets of preaching as spiritual direction, but one characteristic pervades all three sermons—that of guiding congregations to discern the palpable presence of God in their midst. This preoccupation with God serves as a method for revealing the holy in the ordinary, assisting the people of God to find God always, in all ways. This approach foregrounds a sacramental understanding of life, of the sermon, and of the congregation, as well as of the grace-filled presence for which we hunger and thirst. Small details have been changed in the sermons from their original delivery for publication purposes.

Over time, I have developed a method for laying sermons upon the page so that their contemplative spirit is experienced. These space-filled texts make room for God and for quiet, organizing delivery pace and intensity. My hope is that because of the architecture of words arranged in *real* space on the page—my readers here are able to hear and experience the sermon not only as a textual event—but also as an oral/aural event, and a spiritual event, as well. Through trial and error I have found that a sermon swept up into the tightly knit form of paragraphs and grammar (which is vital to writing that intends to be *read*) is not helpful for writing whose purpose is *delivery*. In the end there is no good solution to a sermon's being reduced to a written page.

Finally, allow me to offer a cautionary note regarding the idiosyncratic punctuation found within these sermons. After having spent the better part of a lifetime with Emily Dickinson's poetry, her rather bizarre punctuation—which notes pace and delivery (intonation, too), more than grammar—deeply influenced me and how I *hear* on a page. Dashes are delivery cues, denoting a short, unpredictable pause (unanticipated by the congregation) which heightens anticipation. The ellipses (…) indicate an active stretching of time (or *ritardando*) before proceeding. Space between words can be literally translated as the brief moment of silence during which one's eye traverses the space between the two words.

Ideally, the sermon's visual lay-out is a sound-map: one "hears" how it sounds because the eye *sees* it. A sermon can be heard, then, even though one is limited to silently reading the text.

Sermon One: Go Find Your Greatness!

My model of preaching as spiritual direction proposes that sermons will self-consciously, explicitly guide individuals and congregations in their need for vocational formation. This sermon was preached for Drury University's (Christian) Baccalaureate service, in Springfield, Missouri, on May 16, 2004. As guest preacher for this occasion I was offered a rare and wonderful moment, namely, a chapel filled with students only sixty minutes away from their official launch into the "real world." This sermon's ultimate aim was that of inspiriting these almost-graduates into conscientious consideration of the kind of persons God was calling them to "be," that is, to their *vocation* of becoming. This sermon is self-consciously vocational with the preacher understanding herself as an expressly Christian and *religious* voice during a weekend filled with graduation celebrations.

A foundational criterion for preaching as spiritual direction lies in drawing our attention always—and in all ways—to God.

This sermon's penultimate aim was that of seeking to provide a theological grounding for the graduates' lives, particularly God's need of them.

Text: Wisdom of Solomon 7:22-30

For my mother[1]

This great day of accomplishment began . . . years ago . . . remember "phonics"? Then multiplication tables, rote memorization, Saxon math, McDougall math, workbooks, test taking strategies, ACTs, GPA, IQ, EQ, PSAT, GRE, LSAT, MCAT, GMAT . . .[2] and the list goes on. For as long as there has been teaching and learning—scholars from Socrates to John Dewey to Harold Bloom have debated *how best* to teach, and then even more complicated—how to evaluate aptitude for learning—and most complicated of all, how to measure what has been "learned."

And then? There's another category apart from all the others: wisdom. Beyond our abilities in calculus or our capacities to score well on a test or "to play well with others" . . . lies the elusive, more valuable virtue: wisdom.

How do we get *that*?

When my sisters and I were little girls, every time we closed the backdoor behind us—as we left home to walk to school— Mom called out the door after us,

"*Girls!* GIRLS! Go find your greatness!"

My sisters and I would look at one another and roll our eyes—*all we were hoping for—was to survive one more day of* school at Western Oaks Elementary—and our mom? Well, our mom—was literally calling us to imagine a future—and prepare for it—when that was the farthest thing from our minds . . . .

This is what wisdom does. She calls to us. Every morning as we shut the door behind us—pile into the car—on the way to work, or graduate school, or a brand-new career—

In the midst of all the chaos and activity . . . wisdom calls to us. Poking a hole in our virtually shrink-wrapped patterns of existence—beyond our preoccupations with:

what others think about us
  or how well we're measuring up
    beyond worries about having enough money
      and how our lives will turn out.

Across all our preoccupations
  wisdom calls to us—
    reminding us:
      Go! Find your *greatness*.

Graduates: the people you love—and who love you—are going to ask about your career goals, marriage, and future income potential, and possibly . . . your intentions regarding fame!—with your best interests at heart they will ask you dozens of questions about what you plan to "do" with your college degree and your life . . . and that's OK . . .

But the work of God this morning—is to ask a different question: What kind of human person—are you going to "be"?

It's not only about what you're going to "do" with your life . . . but: Who are you going to *become?*

Consider pursuing wisdom—at all costs—for God loves nothing so much as the person who lives with wisdom.

So while it is the work of your family and peers to torment you lovingly with unanswerable questions about your career—the deeper question, "To what shall I devote my life?" persists—

This question is a vocational question involving not only our occupation . . .
  but *who* we love—and how and why,
    how we spend our resources—
      and the risks we are willing to take for one another's well-being—

Walter Brueggemann puts it this way: "Vocation is begun in the moments when we find our purpose for being in the world is related to the purposes of God."[3]

As certainly as the tides pull the ocean, there is within each of us an elusive yet unyielding pull toward God's purposes in our lives . . . a longing to find not just a job—or a future—but our vocation, to discover our specific role in God's purposefulness in creation.

It begins with seeking wisdom. And we *get* wisdom through the hard work of—"finding our greatness."

But what is greatness?

As Americans we associate greatness with: Wealth. Winning sports teams. Fast cars—*big cars:* SUVs. The most friends. Influence and power and . . . large houses—and really, really white (no, make that the *whitest*) teeth.

Our American preoccupation with celebrity-ism (misunderstood as greatness) explains why millions of us glue our noses to the TV screen every week for *Survivor* and *The Bachelor* to distract us. These so-called reality shows bathe us in candy-coated—artificial *celebrity* fame; not greatness.

And then by contrast, we've all seen spectacular achievement and its well-deserved fame. Did you see Sally Ride become the first woman in space? Did you see Mother Teresa accept the Nobel Peace Prize? Did you hear about Eleanor Roosevelt's address to the League of Nations? Do you remember Harriet Tubman's underground railroad? Did you read the words of Abraham Lincoln's Emancipation Proclamation? Have you heard of Cesar Chavez's astounding work toward liberating migrant workers?

These are extraordinary human beings with extraordinary minds and talents. But what about *us*? More—*ordinary* people *like us* seeking greatness?

Martin Luther King Jr. said that we cannot all be famous but we can all be great.

What *is* this *greatness*?! for ordinary folks—like us?
Come away with me—for a moment: from Springfield to

Dallas-Fort Worth International Airport, to New York City—to Tel Aviv—to Jerusalem, where:

This morning—before dawn—a group of Israeli women arose—and made their way to border-patrol checkpoints—to stand all day in the blistering desert sun.

These Israeli women stand next to Israeli border guards *not as their allies* but as protectors of the Palestinian women whom those Israeli border guards will search . . . every day. This group of amazing Israeli women keeps watch in the desert—ensuring the dignity and well-being of their so-called enemies.

Machsom Watch is the name of their organization. It began as a response to the second intifada in September of 2000—and continues to this day.[4]

Imagine! This moment, while we worship peacefully, as we breathe in—and breathe out—the celebration of this day, those Israeli women are standing watch in the desert . . .

They decided that since their national leaders seem incapable of *making* peace—it was their work to *seek* peace.

Not one of those women is famous—or has been featured on the front page of the *New York Times*. Millions of us are not clambering to watch them on T.V.

And—is their work for peace "*successful*"?—the briefest glance at any newspaper confirms escalating violence in the Middle East.

Are these peace-seeking Israeli women . . . *wise*, really?

That's the problem with wisdom and *greatness*. They often appear foolish.

In the sixteenth century, Galileo, in a letter to his friend Johannes Kepler, admits that he had long agreed with Copernicus—that the earth rotated around the sun—but had been afraid to say so for fear he would be laughed at.

Finding our greatness means—we may appear foolish.

Like those *Israeli* women seeking peace by protecting the bodies of—*Palestinian* women. A small, small, drop of peace . . . in the sea of violent trouble that is the Middle East.

But Jesus was profoundly preoccupied with the small. Whether it was a mustard seed or Zacchaeus. Jesus' kin-dom is the opposite of super sized—just five small loaves were enough to feed thousands. Jesus' entire life reads in small print, really . . .

And then there's God. God is even more emphatic than Jesus when it comes to preferring the small. When it was time to alter the world—an *infant* appeared.

Social philosopher Hannah Arendt observed what we all feel—that each and every child is the birth of the new—she spoke of it as "natality"[5]—that is, each child enacts the utterly *new* in the universe—including possible release from present oppressions!

I promise you, graduates, that on this day as you await your diploma—your parents are remembering the day you were born as they snuggled you—a mere infant—in their arms, their prayers were filled with *hopes* of natality—

Greatness. They had in mind for you: *greatness.*

Last spring the great civil rights leader and president of the National Association for the Advancement of Colored People, Julian Bond, spoke in Tulsa. Immediately following Bond's lecture, someone asked him, "You have devoted over fifty years of your life to this struggle, and so little has changed—how on earth do you keep your hope?"

Mr. Bond thought several moments then said, "You know I was in Los Angeles and a student there showed me a photo of Rodney King being beaten, then of the riots that followed, and this student said to me, 'Nothing has changed in America'."

"And I had to correct him. Back in the days of the civil rights protests there was a Rodney King being beaten—or lynched—on every other corner. And nobody was taking a picture of it. And even if they had—nobody would have taken notice."

Bond continued: "There is progress. There is progress every time one of us says 'no' to bad behavior. It's that simple and that profound. Stand up. Stand up and speak to the behavior! Because things *do* change."[6]

Hard to imagine anything smaller than standing up and saying no to bad behavior. All it takes is our voice. Our voices saying, "*No!*"

Have you heard about the three U.S. soldiers serving at Abu Ghraib who stood up and said no to the mistreatment of Iraqi detainees? *Their* names are worthy of remembering: David Sutton, William Kimbro, and Joseph Darby. They refused orders to participate in the abuse. The *New York Times* broke this story of three men who stood up and said no to bad behavior, as Julian Bond challenged us to do.

In the same article, the *Times* noted: ". . . for many years scholars have pondered the odd ethical individual" but psychologists believe such persons are guided by a "strong moral compass" and previous experiences in "determining their own destiny" through "enduring whatever negative consequences might come from their actions."[7] Small acts of saying no along the way made these men capable of saying no under great pressure.

Small acts—small yet *profound* behaviors—grow us. They *make room in us*—a place capable of real commitment, of risk, risking ourselves for one another, for justice—*and* for God's purposes in our lives . . .

When God seeks to change human history God doesn't do it from the outside—as if pulling some strings—but God enters into history, through the risk of birth—and the risk of freedom—God enters into history—through our lives.

Theologian Douglas John Hall uses the analogy of a musical score—to explain how God works in this world. God changes the world—like a composer adding a new voice to an orchestral score. Add a new voice? It changes *everything.*[8]

This morning—if you are not already reassured or convinced by any of my words, be most compelled by these:

You are the voice, *yours is the voice* God is counting on—to change the course of events in the lives of human persons, communities, churches, the world—and creation itself.

God depends on you finding your way to wisdom through finding your greatness—in small, foolish, courageous ways that make your voices *strong.*

God does not intervene in history through acts of dominating power, or omniscient thunderbolts. No. But through an *infant* whose voice, whose words, rewrote the future.

That's what God does in human history. God changes history—transforming it—with a voice . . .

and so graduates—it is time.
Go!

Find Your Greatness!!

Because God *needs your* voice to change the world.

GO!!!!!

Sermon Two: A Listening Heart

This sermon was preached for the national gathering of the Association of Disciple Musicians in Fort Worth, Texas, in Robert Carr Chapel on the Texas Christian University campus, July 22, 2007. God and vocational call (of individuals and congregations) are the primary foci of the sermon. The sermon explores desolation as well as apophatic experiences of God. Teresa of Avila makes her presence known, too!

Text: 1 Kings 3:5-12

How do we express the inexpressible: God . . . . . . ? The unutterable, the ineffable, infinite, wordless word that is God?

The history of literature is cluttered with human grasping to express the inexpressible in visions, imagination, images . . . but most especially words that come tumbling out of us . . . from the psalmist to the mystics—to the music of all those gathered today—to my seminarians' papers and ideas and sermons . . . we labor (all of us) to give word to the inexpressible . . .

Like—when my goddaughter (at the time) five years old—Disciple of Christ, Amanda Madigan—played her violin for worship for the first time in her entire five years of life. When Amanda finished playing *All Creatures of Our God and King* for the special music, she returned to her seat, where her mother noticed—Amanda was trembling—

Her mother leaned over and whispered, "Were you nervous?"

"No, Momma, this is not nervous, this is God."

Her mother asked several more questions—wanting to know more about this experience of God that left Amanda trembling . . .

until—finally—

Amanda Madigan—all thirty-seven pounds of her—drew herself up, looked her mother in the eye and said, "Momma! There are no words."[9]

What do we do when there are no words to express this God who causes us to tremble?

We hold the ones we love a little more closely to us . . .

We weep. *We dance!*

We surrender to the wordless Word, trembling.

Spiritual teachers tell us that my goddaughter Amanda's *direct* experience of God in worship—her moment of being utterly *met* by God—yet having no words—is an *apophatic* experience (how's that for a ten-thousand-dollar, seminary word?). Apophatic! To be utterly filled with God and yet wordless. Sacramental theologian Karl Rahner wrote persuasively (what I think we all know in the marrow of our bones) that we are more susceptible to apophatic experience and to God—when we are children.

But experiences of God are not always ecstatic, or infused with the sweet, aching fulfillment—

Take for example those times, in the wee hours of the morning, say 2 A.M., or 3 A.M., or 4 A.M.— we discover ourselves wide awake—as if we'd been startled—not by an *audible* sound— . . . when God calls us in the middle of the night we don't *hear* God so much with our "bodily ears" (as Teresa of Avila noted) but with our *interior* ear—not the inner-ear canal connected with the hammer, anvil, and stirrup bones—but, rather, the interior ear that connects *heart, mind, soul, and strength* . . .

God *does* wake people up (one of God's less endearing habits—many have observed . . .). In those wee hours of the morning—as we lie wide awake, hearts pounding—fears pinning us to our mattresses—(as if draped by a stack of lead aprons like dentists use before x-raying our teeth)—is that *God?* Our minds crowded with worries for children and grandchildren—(and parents and goddaughters), then escalate to worries about job security, and health insurance, and our churches—and without bidding our hearts take flight to the suffering in Darfur, Iraq, Afghanistan; to the five thousand children orphaned by 9/11 and the millions orphaned worldwide from HIV/AIDS—then our restless hearts return to our prayer lists and we walk the hospital halls (in our mind's eye) stopping to pray for those we know by name who are fighting for life and health, and also for all those suffering unto death.

Our pillow, just like the psalmist's, is wet with our tears . . . Can this be God? *Is* this God, then?

Yes. God wakes us up at night. With an invitation just like in the garden of Gethsemane, when Jesus told the disciples, "Wait with me a little while." This sleeplessness when God wakes us to "wait for a while" with the suffering of the world— is unlike Amanda's apophatic experience of being filled with God but having no words. *This* experience of God fills us with words, plenty of them, pouring out of us—and yet we *feel* somehow empty, disconsolate. We feel desolation and yes, God is in it. Not causing it—but waking us up to be with God. . . .

There's another reason, quite different reason God wakes us up beyond that of asking us to "wait for a while," awake to the needs of the world . . .

God *also* wakes us up—to issue a vocational call: calling us to our vocation as *persons* and as congregations.

Maybe the middle of the night—is God's last resort—as we have brilliantly organized God out of our daily lives. Sure, we're church musicians, and pastors, and professors, business folks, attorneys, stay-at-home parents, and deeply committed layfolk—. But though we may *work* for God, and *sing* for God, and *preach* for God and *teach* for God—and show up for God on Sunday—it's often been a very, very long time since we made . . . *room* for God. Poor God. The problem of failing to clear space, make *room* for God is a theme as old as scripture itself—in fact, Advent comes to mind, "No room for the incarnation."

"Poor God" (as my Mom would lament—) . . . [One of my Mother's more eccentric theological bents—was that of poring over dozens of church newsletters each month "searching for evidence of God," as she put it. If—in the course of the newsletter, God had been completely ignored (in favor of church programs and "rah rah sis boom bah," as Mom called it)—Mom took her indelible black-ink, felt-tipped marker and wrote, "Poor God" (followed by a railroad track of exclamation points about a mile long). She tucked these newsletters in the mail to me as a warning against God-less church . . .]. Theologian Douglas John Hall says that when the church gives in to this kind of cultural boosterism, we're no longer living the gospel or learning God.

So *this* God ("Poor God") wakes us out of a deep sleep—guiding us away from "rah rah sis boom bah"—and prodding us toward our vocation.

In the deep silence of the night with only the sound of a dripping faucet—or your baby's breaths in and out . . . —or perhaps the sound of the refrigerator's humming keeping you company, listen. Listen with the ear of your heart, and whisper [to God]— "Speak, Lord, for your servant is listening . . ."

God woke Solomon up in the middle of the night. Solomon's call, like Samuel's—and Jacob's—and so many others—occurs at night.

But at the same time—Solomon's call story is unlike every other call story. When God called Abram—God told Abram *what to do*. And, Moses, too—when God called Moses, God gave Moses a job description. When God called Samuel—God told young Samuel what to *do*.

But when God calls Solomon? Rather than telling Solomon what to *do*, God commands Solomon, "Ask me. Ask me, Solomon, for what you need." That doesn't sound like the God we've known through Genesis, Exodus, Leviticus, Numbers, Deuteronomy, 1 and 2 Samuel. The God—we find in 1 Kings—has a different M.O. God is trying a new approach (and who could blame God?).

"Ask what I should give you," God exhorts Solomon.

Wow. We all know the right answer is if a *genie* asks, "What should I give you?"—the obvious answer is: three more wishes . . .

But when God—asks Solomon—"Ask what I should give you" it's a kind of pop quiz of the wisdom sort.

Solomon—in today's text—was we think—about twenty years old. And responsible for all of Israel's governing. Imagine a twenty-year-old making a bid for the presidency of the United States— . . .

Unbelievably enough—instead of acting like he knew more than he did—Solomon quickly admits to God—all that Solomon *does not know.* I don't even know how to "come in and go out." Or as a lady from the southern states might say, "That poor boy doesn't know which end is up."

So, Solomon asks for "an understanding mind." At least that's how our New Revised Standard Bibles translate what Solomon asked for.

But the Hebrew words that Solomon asked for (literally) are: *lebh shomea* (l-e-b-h s-h-o-m-e-a). A literal translation? Listening heart. Solomon asks for a listening heart. He has an impossible job description—enough worries to keep him up nights for the rest of his life. He doesn't ask for help, for rescue, for relief. But a listening heart.

We—hear the word *heart*—and we translate it as feelings. Hallmark moments. When somebody tells a preacher, "You moved my heart today," the words are usually accompanied by a moist hankie; tears have been shed—that's what we postmoderns mean when we say "heart." It means we *felt* something.

In the ancient Hebrew language of Solomon's time—parts of the body *do* represent feelings: the nose represents anger (ever see an angry person's nostrils flare? My seventh-grade Sunday school teacher's nostrils flared when he was furious with us . . .). The right arm means strength (think about how many times we've read in the Psalms—that God upholds us with "the right arm" [it's the *strong* arm]).

But even though parts of the body—are symbolic for the ancient Israelites—heart is *not the* equivalent of our understanding of heart (love compassion heartsick from grief, etc.) but also the "will or intention." Feelings, thoughts, will—strength—all reside in the Israelites' understanding of "heart."

God does wakes us up, to say, "Ask what I should give you."

Before surrendering to my vocational call to pastoral ministry I was a pianist by profession—living in Tennessee (of all places) where I taught piano lessons to impoverished Appalachian kids for a federal enrichment program—designed to show children living in poverty how many possibilities the world has: starting with music and the piano.

None of my students had pianos at home—in fact, most of them had no running water. No heat source beyond a wood-burning stove. (The fragrance of wood smoke lingered in their clothes—a fragrance I grew to love.)

Sometimes their mommas or daddies would "carry them to church" (as they put it) to practice on a real piano: the church had a piano . . . but typically there was no practicing the piano in between the weekly lessons I provided . . . and my students' progress was . . . well, heartbreakingly slow. Except—except for Becky.

Six weeks into lessons Becky came in, sat down at the school's piano, and played a Bach minuet *perfectly*. The music was pouring out of this child—it wasn't only that the notes were right—she was making *music*.

I asked, "Did your daddy carry you to church to practice?"

"No, Ma'am. My daddy came up here to the school and looked at the piano and he made me a 'play piano' on cardboard that I stretch out across my momma's table and practice on."

It took me a few seconds to visualize what she was telling me: that she practiced on a cardboard (imitation) keyboard—that she unfolded like a map on her mother's kitchen table.

Dumbfounded—I asked, "So Becky, if you can't *hear* the notes you're playing—if the 'play piano' doesn't actually make any sound when your fingers play on it—how exactly did you learn this Bach minuet?"

"Oh, I learnt it by heart, Ma'am," she quickly responded.

The week before—I had played the minuet on the school's piano for Becky "showing her" what it sounded like . . . Becky had listened carefully . . . committing it to that remarkable, powerful place ancient Hebrew people called "the heart."

Becky had learned it from the inside out—using heart, mind, soul, strength, *and will*:

"I learned it by heart, Ma'am."

Next time God wakes you in the middle of the night—there are three good responses:

Seek your vocation, "*Speak Lord, your servant is listening*" might be a good way to begin the conversation, or . . . .

If it seems God is asking, "Will you wait with me a little while," then

stay awake—praying with all your heart, mind, soul, and strength with all those gathered at the heart of suffering that night, or . . .

Perhaps God has woken you to ask, "What do you need me to give you?"

Ask for a listening heart
and then, please, won't you guide us all—to wisdom?

Sermon Three: A Matter of Life and Death

This sermon was the first of four preached for the Barton Clinton Gordey Lecture Series of the great Boston Avenue United Methodist Church in Tulsa, on the first Sunday of Lent (February 17, 2008). The congregation is urged to make room for God through cleaning up the spiritual clutter in our own lives. Meister Eckhart, Teresa of Avila, and Rabbi Zusia supply the voices of wisdom.

Text: Matthew 17:1-8

Remember your first house? Ours—all eight-hundred-and-twenty-five square feet of it—was sheer *perfection*—right here in Tulsa, Oklahoma.

First homes have quite a few surprises though—! Somehow, for example, in the excitement of having found the *perfect home* we failed to notice the furnace was thirty-seven years old—but on the other hand there were terrific surprises, too—and one of the best surprises of *this* home? Neighbors:

Margaret—ninety-two-year-old widow, was our neighbor directly to the south.

Along with Margaret, we had eighty-eight-year-old widow, Mrs. Greenwood (to our north) *and* eighty-two-year-old widow, Hazel—our backyard neighbor to the west. They formed a sort of "holy trinity" of watchful eyes—and unending curiosity—about their new "young" neighbors.

Margaret didn't use the new-fangled technology we call "the telephone." When she wanted to speak with me—she would retrieve from her garage a rake—which, I promise you, was at least as old as Margaret—with only three serviceable tines remaining—and [—when she wanted to speak with me—] Margaret commenced *raking her cement driveway*. Industriously. The sound it produced was something like that of fingernails being scraped against a blackboard.

One evening—when I was pressed for time (I had an elders meeting—and I was trying to finish supper)—Margaret began scraping her driveway. "O for pity's sake," I said to my husband, "I've got to get out there. Margaret wants to talk to me."

I strode across our front yard, and tried the direct approach, "Margaret, you wish to speak to me?"

Margaret stopped raking, and began anxiously wringing her hands. I was a bit alarmed. "Margaret, whatever on earth is the matter?"

She stopped wringing her hands long enough to point accusingly at *my* driveway—asking, "What's all that?"

Relieved, I responded, "Margaret, I've been spring cleaning. All those boxes are filled with things I'm giving away. The American Vets will pick them up tomorrow—but if the boxes are disturbing you, I'll move them into the garage overnight . . ."

"No," she said, "That's not it."

"Then what *is* it, Margaret?"

She looked again at the boxes on my driveway—and she looked at me, shaking her head from side to side with alarm and dismay, saying: "You're far too young to know what to throw away and what to keep!"

I thanked Margaret, went back inside, began washing supper dishes, thinking to myself, "Margaret's right, I *don't* know enough to know *what to throw away—and what to* keep—but, isn't life just like that?—pressing us—always—one step beyond *what* we know—?

Whether it's buying a first home and neglecting to notice the heating system is thirty-seven years old—or that terrifying/

wonderful moment—when you step out of the protective envi-
ronment of the hospital—cradling a newborn in your arms (*your
first*), astounded that you have *no idea*, really—how to be a parent
. . . life consistently, constantly presses us beyond what we know—
"ready or not."

And *Lent*—the Christian season of Lent—asks us

—quite literally, "ready or not," to spend forty days sorting
through what to throw away and what to keep in our *spiritual*
lives.

We *know* why we spring-clean our homes—to give away whatever is perfectly good (and useful to others) that we ourselves,
no longer use. We spring-clean our homes to declutter them,
reclaiming *room* to live—

And so in the same matter, we spend forty days of sorting
through spiritual clutter in our interior lives (during Lent:) to
make room for God.

But paradoxically–making room for God is *not* like adding on
a room to our house—quite the opposite (as fourteenth-century
mystic, Meister Eckhart noted), ". . . God is not found in the soul
by adding anything but by a process of subtraction."[10]

Lent each year—inscribes this question on our hearts: "What
do you need—to *subtract* from your life—to make room for God?"

Maybe it's regret [you need to subtract from your life]—the
regret you carry for something you said—when you were too young
to know better . . . or maybe it's the regret you carry—for what you
did *not* say—in a moment when your courage failed you—

Or maybe *your* spiritual clutter is *resentment*—in the form of
an old, aching grudge that wakes you up like a spiritual back-
spasm—in the middle of the night—

Or is it disappointment . . . ? in yourself . . . or in your kids . . .

Maybe it's with a dream that—although it has ended—you
haven't been able to let go yet . . .

Some of us are all cluttered up with self-pride as tall and
impressive as the Empire State Building . . . *or with pride's opposite:
shame* . . .

Spiritual subtraction is difficult. This is why Lent—urges us to
look at death—unblinking. "From dust you came—to dust you will

return." Lent—points us toward the end of our lives—like a wise, wise sage—asking us to peek behind the curtain of our life and glimpse death—in order to know what to subtract from our lives.

So: Lent asks us to prepare not only for Jesus' death—but for our own death, too. Not in some kind of macabre, crepe-hanging, morose way—*far from it*—we are to be mindful of our death—during Lent—to know *how to live, transfigured—abundantly, in the here and now.*

The history of spirituality—insists our purpose here on earth—is becoming spiritually *free*—so that we grow into exactly what God created each of us—to be. Take Zusia, for instance.

Great rabbis—tell this story of Zusia.

Before his death, Rabbi Zusia wept, saying, "In the coming world God will not ask me: 'Why were you not as Moses,' because I am not Moses. God will not ask me: 'Why were you not as Isaiah,' because I am not Isaiah."

"Then why are you weeping?" his disciples asked Rabbi Zusia.

Rabbi Zusia sighed as he answered,

"It is because God will ask me, 'Why were you not Zusia?' Have I lived up to the best that is in me?"[11]

Lent asks us the question, "Have you lived up to the best that is in you?" so we can be transfigured. Which brings us to our Gospel story this morning in which Jesus is quite literally glowing, gaining fuller clarity on what he was living for, why he was here.

There are two details I want us to savor from the transfiguration story this Lent.

First—when the Jewish Christians—to whom the author of Matthew wrote—when they heard that Jesus was on a mountain surrounded by a cloud—they immediately recognized a parallel to Moses glowing with the glory of God on Mount Sinai.

By way of contrast, we—postmodern North Americans—envision *Jesus'* transfiguration as "otherworldly," bringing to mind those Raphael-esque angels (in nineteenth-century paintings) levitating slightly off the ground . . . but Matthew's hearers would *not* have envisioned that—for they knew the glory of the Lord that descended on Moses, was the Hebrew word, *kavod*, which means, heavy, burden—

The glory of God is not only shining and light, not only the Greek word *phos* the writer of Matthew uses—it is—*also* in the very same moment—heavy, *profound.*

The glory of God—is quite simply—dazzling light and heavy burden, transfiguration—with God—is both dazzling light—and heavy burden—for each of us . . . we mustn't presume it will be easy or happen in an instant.

Second, I want for us to savor what the author of Matthew tells us about Jesus' clothes—which—"were dazzling white."

Today—is one of the very few times in scripture that we find the downright postmodern—glitzy word—*dazzling. Dazzling* in the first-century ancient Near East—a time of no electricity; no dazzling marquis—no neon signs—in the midst of a first-century culture in which there was no dazzle. Jesus' clothes were dazzling.

And—they were *white.*

In a time before Clorox bleach, *waaaaaaaay* before seven-hundred-thread-count sheets, *how* is it that Jesus' clothes were dazzling white?

Archaeologists currently excavating an ancient synagogue in the southwestern Golan Heights may have found the answer. Umm el–Kanatir is among the most magnificent—and vast synagogues ever found. Its location is so remote—even looters rarely ventured there—therefore this particular excavation site is remarkably intact—every archaeologists' dream.

But how could the residents of such a poor, remote village have built such a fabulous synagogue? (Kind of like a Boston Avenue Methodist Church popping up in the middle of nowhere—)

Archaeologists found several clues: Umm el–Kanatir was surrounded by a series of pool, fed by fresh water springs. Each of the pools had a small column with a basin on top—as well as bottom drainage. *Inside* the synagogue—archaeologists found a stockpile of limestone pieces with sharp edges. *Outside* the synagogue—archaeologists found—fertile land and evidence of a farming culture—that would have been perfect for growing flax—

The physical work of making flax fibers into dazzling *white* linen required not only repeated pounding with the edges of sharp, limestone pieces—but also repeated rinsing—in limestone water, then clear water. This wealthy synagogue—supplied by fresh water streams and limestone to pound flax into linen—was an economic goldmine—the final product being fine, white linen fibers, woven into the most prized of garments.[12]

Producing dazzling white linen was a monotonous process. A time-consuming process. Pounding flax over and over and over again. Rinsing over and over and over again.

My point is not that Jesus had a robe from the "dazzling coutoure" collection at "Umm el-Kanatir, Ltd." sent special delivery to the mountain for the occasion,

But, rather, that what is revealed in a *moment* with Jesus occurs over the course of a lifetime in you and in me.

And, like today's story, those who know the depth of our transfiguration are only God and a few friends.

My mother—was an early childhood educator who lived her life championing children. She was a kindergarten teacher.

And when, at sixty-six years of age, my mother's oncologist said it was time to stop treatment and call hospice—(from non-Hodgkins lymphoma) my mother beheld me with her beatific, regretful smile—and with unshed tears in her eyes—said,

"I have spent my whole life doing things I didn't entirely know how to do and here I am—at the end of my life—doing something I've never done before! Learning how to die!"

Weeks into the dying process, I walked into my mother's bedroom early one morning where—no longer able to walk or move—Mom asked me,

"Kay Lynn, will you help me with all these boxes?"

"Sure, Mom, what boxes?"

"All these boxes on the bed!"

"Where do you want me to put them, Mom?"

"Well, how about I hand them to you and you carry them into my closet and put them on those overhead shelves above my hang-up clothes."

So I began to carry imaginary boxes—from bed to closet—making round trip after round trip, each time Mom would "hand" off more boxes to be stored—

After a few minutes, Mom said,

"There aren't any boxes, are there?"

"No, Mom." We burst out laughing—finally when we were *both* weak from laughter she said,

"I'm having one of those . . . you told me about them last week . . ."

"Hallucinations, Mom."

"Right. I'm having a hallucination. But would you mind helping me with the rest of these boxes!"

I kept carrying boxes to the closet. Who knows? Maybe Mom was doing some spring cleaning—getting rid of last bits of spiritual clutter—before she died—subtracting . . . to make more room for God.

Later that same week, Mom called me into her room,

"Kay Lynn—you have *got* to do something about all these children under my bed! I'm worried about them. I want you and your sister to take them—all of them—outside. They need sunlight and fresh air. Feed them a good lunch. I'm going to rest while you and your sister take care of these children. I just *love* having them but I'm too tired."

My sister and I—shooed all the children out from under Mom's bed—and then "took them outside" for the day.

The last words my Mom spoke to me were these:

"Kay Lynn, I love you . . . there is the most darling little boy still here—holding my hand. He is such a comfort to me. I think I'll let him stay."

This is the transfiguring wisdom of Lent: we die the way we live.

Don't mishear me—I don't mean the easiness or difficulty of our dying—is determined by our living. My mother's death was a difficult one—

but

In her death
My mother—a woman who gave her life to children—

was cared for—and kept company by children–
And her transfiguring love
became fully visible to all those around her
.... *dazzlingly* so.

May it be so with you . . . and *you* . . . and you—and you, and
you, *and you all* [gesture—entire congregation], as well. Amen.

APPENDIX 1
SERMON PREPARATION

THE PRIMARY SOURCE FOR ALL PREACHING IS, OF COURSE, Scripture. It is presumed and hoped the preacher will follow the lectionary, excepting when congregational matters of spiritual and/ or intellectual development, or national and international crises necessarily guide the pastor, temporarily, away from the lectionary. It is also presumed, as has been said earlier, that pastors bring various rhetorical and textual criticisms to bear upon their interpretive work, such as historical-critical, literary, and form criticism, as well as feminist, womanist, postcolonialist, and other theories of criticism.

I. Precritical Naïveté: Contemplation*

However, sermon preparation for preaching as spiritual direction *begins* (each Monday) with a contemplative, "precritical naïveté" process. This precritical process is shaped by contemplative prayer and imagination, particularly *lectio divina,* that is, sacred reading. This first movement of sermon preparation, itself a form of guided meditation, may initially, for a "newcomer," require the better part of two hours' time. As one grows more accustomed to *lectio* and *examen* the actual spent time lessens, as the preacher's attentive skills and "noticing God acumen" increase.

During the precritical stage of sermon preparation the "text" being examined is that of the preacher's (and congregation's) life.

---

*This is a composite of materials guiding the exegetical process, based upon the work of my teacher Mary Margaret Pazdan and my colleague Joseph Jeter, Jr., as well as Ignatian *examen.*

In this first movement of sermon preparation, the preacher meditates upon his or her current relationship with God, others, and the world. The "exegetical guide" below combines the ancient art of *lectio divina* with a less ancient practice developed by Ignatius of Loyola, known as *examen*. This critically important, first formation step in the overall exegetical process of preaching as spiritual direction focuses affective attention upon not only the "text" of one's life but also the congregation's life. Momentarily, but only momentarily, strictly *critical* engagement is suspended as is the actual scriptural text to be preached. "Felt experience" is privileged, as are emotions and felt concerns. The preacher listens deeply for the Spirit's guidance:

A. Reflect on how you are in relationship with God, your congregation, the world:
- Open yourself to God's presence, practice stillness.
- Quieten yourself, breathe.
- Recognize concerns: articulate "free-floating" anxiety and stressors.
- Where did you encounter God in the everyday events of "ordinary life" in this past week: in your family, your congregation, your time in prayer?
- Did you feel God at work in misunderstandings, fears, pain, joy?
- Spend some time with the blessings and concerns of your denominational and/or ecclesial "home."
- Recognize concerns in political arenas, places of violence and hope.
- Reflect on the blessings and concerns within the liturgical cycle.
- Reflect on blessings within the earthly cycle.

B. Reflect on your congregation:
- Where have you glimpsed God at work in the everyday events of "ordinary life" within the congregation this past week?
- Where have you felt God prompting you or nudging you in regard to your congregation's formation and purposefulness?
- What about God's absence? Where? When?
- How has the congregation embodied Christ's presence this past week? Where? When? To whom?

- Reflect on the spiritual well-being of the children and teenagers in your congregation. Where/when have you glimpsed them (individually or as a group) embody Christ's presence this past week?
- What are this congregation's particular gifts? How might you "show" these gifts to the congregation?

II. Precritical Scriptural Naïveté

The next, proceeding movement of the exegetical process seeks to mend the head/heart, cognitive/affective split that, though very necessary initially for critical reflection and thinking upon one's faith, all too often, and quite unhappily, remain "split" following the pastor's theological education. There is no cause for anxiety, however, that the process of preparing sermons for preaching as spiritual direction will minimize the important critical work of exegesis taught in seminaries and divinity schools. The critical aspects of sermon preparation will quickly follow those of precritical! Before engaging in the critical dimensions of exegetical preparation, though, it is essential for the preacher as spiritual director to engage in one further set of "precritical" activities—this time, those related directly to the scriptural text (or texts) on which the sermon will be based. In doing so, the preacher will be mending some gaps: gaps between mind and heart, intellect and spirit, scholarship and spirituality mentioned in the first chapter of this book.

A. Pray over the text:
- In solitude and complete silence, read the text with the full force of your attention; take your time, give it space to breathe and to speak.
- Read the text with, as Benedict advised, the "ear of your heart."
- Read the text out loud with a full one-second stop (silent) in between each word. Which word or phrase "moves your heart?"
- Get up. *Move!* Walk the text. Sing the text. Chant the text. If you're a swimmer: *swim* the text!
- Read the text again—with as many translations as you can gather.

- Read the text as if your congregation's life *depends* upon it (it does . . .).

B. Begin to listen for *intuitive* connections:
- What questions float to the surface?
- What memories are brought up? Childhood memories? Teen memories? Adult? Congregational memories?
- What feelings surface in you?
- What can you smell within the text? Feel? Taste? See? Touch?
- What insights are glimpsed?
- What congregational insights surface? Recent history? Long-past history?
- What "picture" or images are evoked? "Preacher, what do you *see*?"[1]

III. Critical Consciousness: Study

Tuesday morning begins the study of the scriptural text: *critical consciousness*. The preacher brings the full force of theological training, textual experts, textual criticisms, historical interpretations, and scholarly research tools to explore the text.
- Gather materials to create new understanding, read widely:
- Identify historical context in which the text came to live, to which it was directed.
- Establish context within the overall book.
- Spend some time in the world of the text.
- Note the important words in the text, know what they mean, how they are used.
- Include most recent commentaries available, biblical dictionaries as well.
- Clearly and simply explain what the author intended this text to do.
- Check a reputable Web site, search for images to download.

IV. Hermeneutic Work: Interpretation
- Make an analogy between our world and the world of the text.
- Does the function of the text in the original setting suggest a function in ours?

- With whom do we identify in the text? (Especially in the New Testament, we preachers, Craddock warns, over-identify with Jesus!)
- What theological points can be made in our setting?
- Where is the integrative bridge between this text and the vocation of your congregation?

V. Making the Connections: Spiritual Direction

Early Wednesday morning, the preacher begins the final aspects of sermon preparation that must be investigated prior to putting pen to paper: making the connections between what has been gleaned through contemplation and study—and the wisdom of spiritual direction.

A. Are any of the themes of spiritual direction evident in the text?

- A call to listen "with the ear of the heart?"
- A call to "Behold! God!"?
- A call to "Wake up!" and consciously co-create life with God?
- A call to develop vocational matters? Individually? Relationally? Congregationally?
- A call to see each moment of "ordinary life" as sacramental? Holy?
- A call to focus on seeing "as God sees"?

B. What, if any, classical texts of Western spirituality surface in "conversation" with the scriptural texts?

- Sayings of the Desert Fathers or Mothers?
- Writings of mystics?
- Benedict's *Rule*? Gregory's *Pastoral Care*?
- Writings and/or sermons of the Reformers?

C. What, if any, issues interface with the scriptural text among the interdependent pairs[2] of spiritual life?

- Receptivity/activity.
- Desolation/consolation.
- Attachment/detachment.

VI. Making Room for the Holy Spirit and Writing

It is now time for the preacher to think *indirectly* about the sermon while, as my spiritual director would say, waiting to "see what surfaces" from among all the pages of insights and scholarship gained from the previous five movements of preparation. Both the sermon and preacher are now at the mercy of the Holy Spirit, which, paradoxically enough, has best access to engage the preacher when the preacher is alone—outdoors—engaged in *another* activity. It is quite literally time to mow the lawn, or weed the garden, or go for on a walk.[3] This sixth movement in the exegetical guide for preaching as spiritual direction may seem less important than those of the precritical and critical moments, particularly when the preacher is feeling hurried. But allowing the preparation to lie fallow—even for a few hours—inevitably surfaces the more salient aspects to be included in the sermon.

At this time in the process the preacher engages the "brilliant luminaries of homiletic method," mentioned in chapter 1, regarding the sermon's architecture and structure.

VII. Performance

The final aspect of preparing for preaching as spiritual direction is, like for all sermons, that of performance. At this point in the preparation, the sermon must be written (though certainly, some preachers will choose to preach without notes), selecting relevant fruits among the harvest gleaned through the six-step exegetical process.

Preaching as spiritual direction presumes, as emphasized earlier, that the preacher is "God-person and guide" of (and for) the congregation. Most typically this "God-person" is moved to preach each Sunday by the depth of concern she or he has for the congregation and its vocation. It follows that the voice of such preachers is a very natural, conversational tone. "Stained-glass" intonations, or chiding—or, heaven forbid, saccharine-sweet, sing-song vocal delivery—is not consonant with preaching as spiritual direction.

Appendix 2

Lectio Divina

LECTIO DIVINA, QUITE LITERALLY TRANSLATED, IS DIVINE reading, a four-step meditation on Scripture first proposed by Carthusian monk Guigo the Great (1140–1193) in his work *The Ladder of Monks*.[1] *Lectio divina* is foundational to spiritual direction as well as to preaching as spiritual direction. Initially designed for individuals, lectio can also be foundational for congregations—and groups like Sunday school classes, or deacons, and youth groups who are seeking God. *Lectio divina* is a method in which one takes the words of Scripture into one's self like a food—not just any food, but the most delectable and delighting of foods, like a melt-in-your-mouth first peach of the summer. In lectio divina the reader "eats" the words of Scripture as surely as the prophet Ezekiel munched on a bit of scroll (Ezek. 3:3).

Lectio is a maddeningly simple yet demanding practice, requiring equal parts art and skill in which the reader becomes the receiver and recipient of Scripture rather than the interpreter of and actor upon the words. In *lectio divina* the affective response is privileged—or at least it is received prior to—the cognitive response, in which words take on shape, context, literary form, meaning. Paul Ricoeur would refer to this encounter as the first naïveté.[2] *Lectio divina* reverses the modern predilection for meaning and information, turning instead to Scripture to receive formation. It is a form of hearing and receiving from the text rather than analyzing or exegeting the text. *Lectio divina* is prior to the exegetical, the "learned" interpretation.

During the process of *lectio divina*—namely, paying attention to and "noticing" God through Scripture—all capacities of human learning are engaged: the senses (feel, smell, imagine the sights, sounds, fragrances, and flavors of the text), one's intellect (thinking as lectio unfolds), one's emotions, insights, and instincts, and one's intuition. That is one reason, in the *lectio* process, that the words of Scripture are read out loud, by one's self! Alone. They need to be spoken, physically felt as one speaks them.

Lectio divina is the entry point to preaching as spiritual direction. *Lectio*'s first step is the preparation of quiet. We resolve to be still. In the stillness, one consciously calls God's presence to mind, emptying one's self of preoccupations and "self-talk" so that instead one might listen to "God-talk.

The second step of *lectio* is that of asking, "God, give me a word," before reading from that day's Scripture. Then, one reads the Scripture—out loud—slowly, with a one-second pause in between each word, so that each word is lifted up out of its embedded, and presumed "meaning." One continues to read in this manner until one's heart is moved by a word, or by a phrase. Because customarily Scripture is not read with our heart while waiting for God to "give us a word" but instead with out intellect, as a means for gathering "meaning" or "information," sometimes the heart is initially reluctant to take up such a foreign practice as reading. But over time, the heart begins to warm up to the new method. And eventually one who has practiced *lectio* can say with confidence at the end of each day's reading, "The word that moved my heart was . . . ," or "The phrase that moved my heart was . . ."

The third aspect for the preacher learning to pray Scripture in the *lectio* method is that of jotting down the word or phrase that has been given, then spending some time meditating on it, or as my spiritual director would say, "sitting with it." Imagine what the word or phrase has to say. Developing where the mind's eye wanders with the word, beginning within self, then meditating on the word while thinking of others, one's congregation, one's community, town, nation, and the world. This moment of meditation on the word, Teresa of Avila advises, is a time to include the imagination, reasoning, will, and intellect.[3]

The final aspect of *lectio* is contemplation, which is quite simply for the preacher, to sit lovingly, quietly gazing at length on the word she/he has been given from Scripture!

NOTES

PREFACE
1. Roman Catholic and Unitarian Universalist faiths are also represented at PTS.

INTRODUCTION
1. German text in Josef Quint, ed. and trans., *Meister Eckharts Traktate,* Die deutschen und lateinischen Werke 5 (Stuttgart: Kohlhammer, 1963), 205. For an alternative translation, see Edmund Colledge and Bernard McGinn, trans., *Meister Eckhart: The Essential Sermons, Commentaries, Treatises, and Defense,* Classics of Western Spirituality (New York: Paulist, 1981), 253.
2. Evelyn Underhill describes such intuitive human knowing as "something most real and fundamental to our human world, permeating all deep human experience, though always lying just beyond the range of conceptual thought." *The Golden Sequence: A Fourfold Study of the Spiritual Life* (New York: Dutton, 1933), 2.
3. Ibid.
4. Ibid.
5. Ibid.
6. Owe Wikström, *The Blinding Darkness* (Örebro: Libris, 1994), 39–40.
7. Margaret Guenther, *Holy Listening: The Art of Spiritual Direction* (Boston: Cowley, 1992), 1.
8. Kathleen Murphy, O.P., quoting Bob Dougherty in a lecture for Spiritual Directors' International annual conference.
9. Jill Clupper, Spiritual Director, Sojourn Training Center in Spiritual Direction.
10. Carolyn Gratton, *The Art of Spiritual Guidance: A Contemporary Approach to Growing in the Spirit* (New York: Crossroad, 1995), 7.
11. Walter Brueggemann, "Covenanting as Human Vocation," *Interpretation* 33 (1979): 126.
12. James Carroll, *Contemplation* (New York: Paulist, 1979), 26.
13. See Douglas John Hall, *Thinking the Faith: Christian Theology in a North American Context* (Minneapolis: Fortress Press, 1991).
14. David Tracy, *The Analogical Imagination: Christian Theology and the Culture of Pluralism* (New York: Crossroad, 1981), 108.
15. Gordon D. Kaufman, *In Face of Mystery: A Constructive Theology* (Cambridge: Harvard University Press, 1993), 408.
16. See Walter Wink, "Prayers and The Powers: History Belongs to the Intercessors," *Sojourners* 19 (October 1990): 10–14.

17. Sin is inattentiveness, laziness—sloth; sin is shame (from feminist thought); sin is avoidance of what is difficult; it is inordinate attachment or addiction. Sin is preoccupation with self-interest that *detracts* or *distracts* from creativity, which suppresses alternative wisdom with that of convention. Sin is a constriction. It represents a warping of or tampering with creativity, a dampening of its life force. Sin is sleepiness and grogginess when Jesus asks, "Wait with me a little while."

18. See Elizabeth A. Johnson, *She Who Is: The Mystery of God in Feminist Theological Discourse* (New York: Herder & Herder, 2002).

19. See, for example, David Tracy's essay, "Theological Method," in *Christian Theology: An Introduction to Its Traditions and Tasks,* ed. Peter C. Hodgson and Robert H. King, 2d ed. (Philadelphia: Fortress Press, 1985), 55.

20. Because of spiritual direction's primary development within the Christian tradition both prior to, and following, the Protestant Reformation, one might think that the practice and application of spiritual direction is strictly limited to a Roman Catholic or at least traditionalist theology and audience. The process of spiritual direction, however, is fully compatible with a wide range of Christian theologies—from evangelical assumptions about the reality of God to feminist, process, panentheistic, and liberationist models—spiritual direction offers, within virtually any theological model, a deeper attention to, and practice of, the presence of God at work in the world.

CHAPTER 1: FORMATION BY ATTRACTION

1. Teresa of Avila, *The Life of Teresa of Avila,* trans. and ed. E. Allison Peers (New York: Doubleday, 1960).

2. This broad and incredibly helpful historical categorization of eras of preaching (from persuasion, to explanation, to communication), is the work of Thomas G. Long, in his book *The Witness of Preaching* (Louisville: Westminster John Knox, 1989), 158–61. I, like so many homileticians, am deeply grateful for and indebted to Professor Long's work. I have added the category of *formation* to his typologies.

3. Father Murray Bodo is a nationally loved and sought-after Franciscan poet and priest, residing in Cincinnati, Ohio.

4. See Mark G. Toulouse, *Joined in Discipleship: The Maturing of an American Religious Movement* (St. Louis: Chalice, 1992), 85; and Long, *Witness of Preaching,* 157–58.

5. Due in part to the influence of John Broadus's *A Treatise on the Preparation and Delivery of Sermons* (New York: Sheldon, 1870).

6. Long, *Witness of Preaching,* 158.

7. Ibid.

8. Fosdick's model and its effects—for good as well as its unintentional negative consequences—will be thoroughly developed in this book's next chapter.

9. Fred B. Craddock's *Preaching* (Nashville: Abingdon, 1985), Eugene L. Lowry's *Homiletical Plot: The Sermon as Narrative Art Form* (Louisville: Westminster John Knox, 2001), and David Buttrick's *Homiletic: Moves and Structures* (Philadelphia: Fortress Press, 1987) remain required reading in every section of the Introduction to Preaching courses I teach at Phillips Theological Seminary. There are, however, a few unintended consequences of preaching as developed by those who crafted the New Homiletic. This book of mine is written in hopes of adding an important missing piece to their amazing body of work. The profound debt owed to these brilliant homileticians is inestimable.

10. Long, *Witness of Preaching.*

11. Ronald J. Allen, *The Teaching Sermon* (Nashville: Abingdon, 1995).

12. Thomas H. Troeger, *Imagining a Sermon* (Nashville: Abingdon, 1990).

13. Carolyn Gratton, *The Art of Spiritual Guidance: A Contemporary Approach to Growing in the Spirit* (New York: Crossroad, 1995), 55–72.

14. Richard Lischer, "Repeat Performance," *Christian Century* 119, no. 18 (August 28, 2002): 22.

15. Eugene Peterson, "The Contemplative Christian: Transparent Lives," *Christian Century* 120, no. 24 (November 29, 2003): 22. Philosophical theologian Nicholas Wolterstorff recently deemed this bifurcation as that between *nonengaged* theology (whose

concern is the academy/speculative) and *engaged* theology (motivated by the church/practical); see his "To Theologians: From One Who Cares about Theology but is Not One of You," *Theological Education* 40, no. 2 (2005): 79–92. Most Protestant seminaries offer courses in spirituality as *elective* courses. Few seminaries *require* courses in spiritual formation for the Master of Divinity degree, however.

16. See John McClure's "Changes in the Authority, Method and Message of Presbyterian Preaching in the 20th Century," in John Mulder, Louis Weeks, and Joe Coalter, eds., *The Confessional Mosaic* (Louisville: Westminster John Knox, 1990), 84–108, esp. 105–08. See also Joseph Faulkner, "What Are They Saying? A Content Analysis of 206 Sermons Preached in the Christian Church (Disciples of Christ) during 1988," in D. Newell Williams, ed., *A Case Study of Mainstream Protestantism: The Disciples' Relation to American Culture, 1880–1989* (St. Louis: Chalice, 1991), 423, 427. Further evidence of God's absence (homiletically speaking) and preaching's failure to speak *formationally* is borne out in the current Lilly Endowment-funded research projects of *Pulpit & Pew* in which *no* current research investigates (1) sermon content analysis, *or* (2) spiritual direction, *or* (3) the formation of pastors.

17. I in no way intend to suggest that *experience* of God trumps or dismisses the invaluable contribution of critical reflection. The images of God we carry with us *shape* our experience of God. Images and perceptions of God must be critiqued. New theologies with their frequently shocking—and uncannily insightful images—must be evaluated and integrated. Our understanding of God will always be partial, always in need of further images and perspectives.

18. Peterson, "The Contemplative Christian," 23.

19. Karl Rahner, *Theological Investigations,* Vol. 8: *Further Theology of the Spiritual Life* 2, trans. David Bourke (New York: Herder & Herder, 1971), 37–43.

20. Gwen Wagstrom Halaas, *Ministerial Health and Wellness Report* (Chicago: Evangelical Lutheran Church in America, 2002), 6, 18. This same report notes on pp. 6, 15, and 42 that while 61 percent of the United States' population is obese, 68 percent of ELCA clergy are.

21. All the wandering, leisure, and contemplative prayer occurs, of course, within the life-giving routine of monastic life. Each day begins with Mass. All retreatants are expected to appear for three meals daily. Though complete silence is observed during meals Lebh Shomea interprets communal (silent) meals as corporate activities. The midday *angelus* bell calls us to prayer.

22. Teresa of Avila, *The Life,* XXXVII, 358.

23. Catherine of Siena and Therese of Lisieux complete the trinity.

24. Regarding human failure to practice *openness* to God and the human capacity to *resist* God's attempts to attract us to prayer and attentiveness, Teresa of Avila quipped, "I do not understand what there can be to make [us] afraid, who are afraid to begin mental prayer, nor do I know what it is [we] dread. The Devil does well to bring this fear upon us . . ." (*The Life,* VIII, 10). While no one in the twenty-first century construes "The Devil" as Teresa did in her medieval worldview, it is conceivable even to a theologically, well-educated, postmodern mind that a "power or principality" could actively kindle *resistance* to praying; see Wink, "Prayers and The Powers," *Sojourners* 19 (October 1990): 10–14.

25. Evagrius Ponticus, *Praktikos* 92, in *The Praktikos: Chapters on Prayer,* ed. and trans. John Etudes Bamberger, Cistercian Studies Series 4 (Spencer, Mass.: Cistercian Publications, 1970), 39.

26. Margaret R. Miles, *Image as Insight: Visual Understanding in Western Christianity and Secular Culture* (Boston: Beacon, 1985).

27. Ibid., 141.

28. Paul Tillich, *Systematic Theology,* Vol. 1 (Chicago: University of Chicago Press, 1951), 121.

29. Roman Catholics understand seven sacraments as channels of grace, encounters with Christ and therefore, a meeting with God. The Second Vatican Council broadened the understanding of sacrament to include the church, that is, "the community of all those persons who belong to Christ" (Thomas N. Hart, *The Art of*

Christian Listening [New York: Paulist, 1980], 6, citing *Constitution on the Church*, #1). I mean to suggest that preaching be considered an encounter that *is* sacramental—God is somehow present and at work in it and by extension, God is present and at work through the preacher—through the preacher's listening for (and with) God on behalf of the congregation.

30. See Timothy Fry, ed., *RB 1980: The Rule of St. Benedict in Latin and English with Notes* (Collegeville, Minn.: Liturgical, 1981), chaps. 39–40 and prologue, p. 49.

31. Ibid., 173–80.

32. Teresa of Avila, *The Life*, VIII, 7.

33. Ibid., VIII, 2.

34. George Herbert, *The Country Parson, The Temple*, Classics of Western Spirituality, ed. John N. Wall Jr. (New York: Paulist, 1981).

35. Ibid., 62.

36. Ibid., 63.

37. Ibid., 281.

38. Ibid., 7.

39. Ibid.

40. Ibid., xiv.

41. See Long, *Witness of Preaching*, 19–47.

42. That preaching's purpose is that of the spiritual formation of individuals and communities of faith reaches across the dramatically diverse theological and denominational contexts of the twenty-first century and also the hugely diverse span of class, race, gender, sexual orientation, age, and ecclesiology in our current context. Congregations, whether first-generation Hispanic Disciples of Christ or open and affirming United Churches of Christ or Korean Presbyterian churches (or fill in the blank) *need* spiritual formation and guidance in seeking God always in all ways.

43. Gender-exclusive texts will retain their historic voice throughout this book. Alan of Lille, *The Art of Preaching* (Kalamazoo, Mich.: Cistercian Publications, 1981), 16–17.

44. Irenaeus, *Against Heresies* IV.20.7, translation as given in *Catechism of the Catholic Church*, 2d ed. (Vatican City: Libreria Editrice Vaticana, 2000), 77 (no. 294).

CHAPTER 2: FORMATIONAL VOICE-PRINTS

1. Numerically speaking, Western Oaks Christian Church (Disciple of Christ), in Oklahoma City, Oklahoma, was among the fastest growing Disciple congregations in the Oklahoma Region for several years in the 1970s, scarcely what was expected of a congregation with a pastor who is paraplegic.

2. Mary Lin Hudson and Mary Donovan Turner, *Saved From Silence: Finding Women's Voice in Preaching* (St. Louis: Chalice, 1999), 9.

3. The formational voice-print for Jesus' disciples was, no doubt, Jesus.

4. Alan of Lille, *The Art of Preaching* (Kalamazoo, Mich.: Cistercian Publications, 1981), 16–17.

5. Richard Lischer, *The Company of Preachers: Wisdom on Preaching, Augustine to the Present* (Grand Rapids: Eerdmans, 2002), 3.

6. Fred B. Craddock, *As One Without Authority: Essays on Inductive Preaching* (Enid, Okla.: Phillips University Press, 1971).

7. Craddock reiterated this fundamental purpose of his scholarship, writing, and teaching in a May 2008 visit to Phillips Theological Seminary to preach for graduation.

8. Granted, it is only with decades of ecumenical and social justice work that religious texts previously understood as protected domains of their specific communion have become shared.

9. Again, it is necessary to emphasize that I am speaking here of mainstream, primarily Caucasian congregations.

10. Austin Phelps, *The Theory of Preaching: Lectures on Homiletics* (New York: Scribners, 1882).

11. Roxanne Mountford, *The Gendered Pulpit: Preaching in American Protestant Spaces* (Carbondale, Ill.: Southern Illinois University Press, 2003), 60.

12. Austin Phelps, *Men and Books: or Studies in Homiletics, 1882* (New York: Scribners, 1992), iii.

13. Because of their influence and popularity, the preaching treatises of Phelps and Broadus became, according to Mountford, "uniquely targeted by contemporary scholars and preachers for criticism." Mountford continues: "In his essay, 'Is There Still Room for Rhetoric' Fred B. Craddock . . . argues that Broadus, like Phelps and many other sacred rhetoricians of the nineteenth century, contributed to the deductive, three-point sermon, which began with the explication of sacred texts, moved on to apply the text to everyday life, and fully concluded with an appeal to the will, a pattern based on the assumption of the superior moral knowledge of the preacher" (*The Gendered Pulpit*, 60).

14. Robert Moats Miller, "Fosdick, Harry Emerson," in William Willimon and Richard Lischer, eds., *Concise Encyclopedia of Preaching* (Louisville: Westminster John Knox, 1999), 154.

15. O. C. Edwards Jr., "History of Preaching," in Willimon and Lischer, *Concise Encyclopedia of Preaching*, 223.

16. Miller, "Fosdick," 154.

17. Harry Emerson Fosdick, *Living Under Tension: Sermons on Christianity Today* (New York: Harper & Bros., 1941), 141.

18. Cited in Lionel Crocker, ed., *Harry Emerson Fosdick's Art of Preaching: An Anthology* (Springfield, Ill.: Charles C. Thomas, 1971), 29.

19. Edwards, "History of Preaching," 223.

20. Edmund Holt Linn, *Preaching as Counseling: The Unique Method of Harry Emerson Fosdick* (Valley Forge: Judson, 1966), 13.

21. Cited in ibid., 13 n.2.

22. Ibid., 16.

23. Ibid.

24. "Missional" in the sense of the church's purposefulness, *not* in the postcolonial understanding of mission.

25. Harry Emerson Fosdick, *On Being Fit to Live With: Sermons on Post-War Christianity* (New York: Harper & Bros., 1946), 145, emphasis added.

26. Linn, *Preaching as Counseling*, 25.

27. Don S. Browning, *The Moral Context of Pastoral Care* (Philadelphia: Westminster, 1976), 19.

28. Ibid., 17–18, emphasis added.

29. Even though Reinhold Niebuhr and his students (including Langdon Gilkey) had been criticizing the myth of progress for at least thirty years prior to Browning's work, progress in the area of the psychological "self" proved more resistant (than in the culture at large) to theological critique.

30. There is one exception to this. Teresa of Calcutta is oft quoted in student sermons. I'm not certain why—except that she is contemporary so my students (who have been formed by media-driven culture rather than by print) have been *visually* exposed to her, her life, and her mission through television. By way of comparison, Teresa of Avila (who is decidedly *not* visually communicated via media) is virtually unknown by my students.

31. By way of anecdotal example, during my high school years (when Browning's book *The Moral Context of Pastoral Care* was being written), my Disciples of Christ pastor preached a series of sermons based on *Jonathan Livingston Seagull*. *Jonathan Livingston Seagull* was a phenomenon that, like a drop of food coloring in a glass of water, permeated American middle-class white culture. It proclaimed the gospel of self-realization and self-actualization, both tapping into and cultivating an American hunger for individual freedom *from* a herd or flock mentality—yet without articulating a freedom *for* anything beyond its own transcendent freedom.

That same pastor was baffled when the congregation soundly defeated his proposal that the church building be made available for daily use by the community senior citizens' day center. Basic Christian virtues of justice sharing had so long been neglected that our responsibility to our neighbors in need had been negatively affected.

If only my pastor had explored Benedict's *Rule* and it practices of Christian community and hospitality! Such a specifically Christian text could have been brought to bear upon the more familiar secular *Seagull* text, providing a much-needed Christian critique of utilizing the church's resources exclusively for church members.

32. Browning, *The Moral Context of Pastoral Care*, 107.

33. Thomas G. Long, *The Witness of Preaching* (Louisville: Westminster John Knox, 1989), 32.

34. Douglas John Hall, *Thinking the Faith: Christian Theology in a North American Context* (Minneapolis: Fortress Press, 1991), 158–69.

35. Paul Tillich, *Systematic Theology*, Vol. 1 (Chicago: University of Chicago Press, 1951), 71–81.

36. See, for example, Langdon Gilkey's description of life within an internment camp in *Shantung Compound: The Story of Men and Women Under Pressure* (San Francisco: Harper & Row, 1966), especially chap. 6.

37. John McKnight, *The Careless Society: Community and Counterfeits* (New York: HarperCollins, 1995), 36–52.

38. See Hall, *Thinking the Faith*, 169–96.

39. See Julian of Norwich, *Showings*, trans. Edmund Colledge and James Walsh, The Classics of Western Spirituality (New York: Paulist, 1978).

40. See McKnight, *The Careless Society*, 43–52.

41. Margaret Guenther, *Holy Listening: The Art of Spiritual Direction* (Boston: Cowley, 1992), x.

42. Ibid.

43. Carolyn Gratton, *The Art of Spiritual Guidance: A Contemporary Approach to Growing in the Spirit* (New York: Crossroad, 1995), 199 n.1.

44. Berrigan and other religious professed (and lay Catholics) protest the build-up of the United State's military industrial complex and the proliferation of nuclear arms by illegally entering nuclear production facilities. Having gained entrance the protestors hammer against the impenetrable bombshell's facade then pour human blood upon it (as a sign of the human lives sacrificed by the military complex/nuclear arms build-up).

45. David Tracy, *The Analogical Imagination: Christian Theology and the Culture of Pluralism* (New York: Crossroad, 1981), 108.

46. See, for example, Parker J. Palmer's *Let Your Life Speak: Listening for the Voice of Vocation* (San Francisco: Jossey-Bass, 2000).

47. Teresa of Avila, *The Way of Perfection* (New York, Doubleday, 1964), 55.

48. See Steven Webb, *The Gifting of God: A Trinitarian Ethics of Excess* (New York: Oxford University Press, 1996).

49. See William Paulsell's *Disciples at Prayer: The Spirituality of the Christian Church (Disciples of Christ)* (St. Louis: Chalice, 1995); Amy Hollywood's *The Soul as Virgin Wife: Mechthild of Magdeburg, Marguerite Porete, and Meister Eckhart* (Notre Dame, Ind.: University of Notre Dame Press, 1995); and Gregory L. Jones and Stephanie Paulsell's *The Scope of Our Art: The Vocation of the Theological Teacher* (Grand Rapids: Eedrmans, 2001), all of which are beginning to retrieve the classics of the common Christian tradition.

50. Douglas John Hall, *God and Human Suffering: An Exercise in the Theology of the Cross* (Minneapolis: Augsburg, 1986), 49–71.

51. Ibid., 31–48.

52. My theology of attraction parallels Hall's theology regarding God's commitment to the world.

53. Evelyn Underhill, *The Spiritual Life: Great Spiritual Truths for Everyday Life* (Oxford: Oneworld, 1993), 16–19, 27.

54. See M. Basil Pennington, *Thomas Merton Brother Monk: The Quest for True Freedom* (New York: Continuum, 1997), 14–38.

CHAPTER 3: MINDING THE FORMATIONAL GAPS

1. Teresa of Avila, *The Interior Castle*, Classics of Western Spirituality, trans. Kieran Kavanaugh and Otilio Rodriguez (New York: Paulist, 1979), 35.

2. Anthony Padovano, *Free to Be Faithful* (Paramus, N.J.: Paulist, 1972), 31.

3. Barbara Brown Taylor, *The Preaching Life* (Cambridge: Cowley, 1993), 49.

4. John Wilkins, *Ecclesiastes: Or A Discourse Concerning the Gift of Preaching as it Falls Under the Rule of Art*. (London: S. Gellibrand, 1646), 14.

5. Roxanne Mountford, *The Gendered Pulpit: Preaching in American Protestant Spaces* (Carbondale, Ill.: Southern Illinois University Press, 2003), 47.

6. See Phillips Brooks, *Lectures on Preaching: Delivered before the Divinity School of Yale College in January and February, 1877* (New York: Dutton, 1877).

7. William Hethcock, "Phillips Brooks," in William Willimon and Richard Lischer, eds., *Concise Encyclopedia of Preaching* (Louisville: Westminster John Knox, 1999), 46–48.

8. See Mountford, *The Gendered Pulpit*, 60–63.

9. Mike Regele, *Death of the Church* (Grand Rapids: Zondervan, 1995), 206.

10. Janet Ruffing, "Sevenfold Results in the Direction Relationship that Signifies the Work of the Holy Spirit" (Paper delivered at the Annual Conference of Spiritual Directors International, 1994).

11. Francis of Assisi (described by many as the first modern saint) preached to an era associated, like postmodernity, with sweeping change. Along with his reforming ethos toward Mother Church, Francis brought a reforming spirit to preaching. *The Legend of the Three Companions* demonstrates that Francis was more interested in the language of sincerity than in rhetoric. My insistence on authenticity and *transparency* are deeply influenced by Francis' model of preaching. See Jacques Le Goff, *Saint Francis of Assisi*, trans. Christine Rhone (London: Routledge, 1999), 118.

12. Margaret R. Miles, *Image as Insight: Visual Understanding in Western Christianity and Secular Culture* (Boston: Beacon, 1985), 142. See also chap. 1, above.

13. Ruffing, "Sevenfold Results."

14. Benedicta Ward, trans., *The Sayings of the Desert Fathers: The Alphabetical Collection* (Kalamazoo, Mich.: Cistercian Publications, 1975), xxii.

15. Ibid., xxi.

16. Ibid.

17. Ibid., xxvi.

18. Ibid., xxvii.

19. Teresa of Calcutta, *The Joy in Loving: A Guide to Daily Living with Mother Teresa* (New York: Penguin, 1996), 403.

20. Laura Swan, *The Forgotten Desert Mothers* (New York: Paulist, 2001), 47.

21. Mary C. Earle, *The Desert Mothers: Spiritual Practices from the Women of the Wilderness* (Harrisburg: Morehouse, 2007), 22.

22. William Harmless, *Desert Christians: An Introduction to the Literature of Early Monasticism* (Oxford: Oxford University Press, 2004), viii.

23. Teresa of Avila, *The Life of Teresa of Avila*, trans. and ed. E. Allison Peers (New York: Doubleday, 1960), VIII, 112.

24. Teresa of Avila, *The Interior Castle*, 43.

25. See Peter G. van Breemen, *As Bread That Is Broken* (Denville, N.J.: Dimension, 1974), 50.

26. Martin Luther, "The Holy and Blessed Sacrament of Baptism," in *Word and Sacrament*, I, ed. E. Theodore Bachmann, *Luther's Works* 35 (Philadelphia: Fortress Press, 1960), 35.

27. Wendy M. Wright, in Reuben P. Job, *A Guide to Spiritual Discernment* (Nashville: Upper Room, 1996), 39.

28. Augustine, *Soliloquies* 2.1.1; translation in *St. Augustin: Homilies on the Gospel of John; Homilies on the First Epistle of John; Soliloquies*, ed. Philip Schaff, *A Select Library of the Nicene and Post-Nicene Fathers of the Christian Church*, Series 1, Vol. 7 (Grand Rapids: Eerdmans, 1978), 547, altered.

29. Teresa of Avila, *The Life*, VII, 97.

30. See Brian Mahan, *Forgetting Ourselves on Purpose: Vocation and the Ethics of Ambition* (San Francisco: Jossey-Bass, 2002).

31. Barbara Brown Taylor, "Buried by Baptism," in *God in Pain: Teaching Sermons on Suffering* (Nashville: Abingdon, 1998), 48.

32. Ibid.

33. Unpublished lecture; for further Merton comments on freedom, see Basil Pennington's *Thomas Merton, Brother Monk: The Quest for True Freedom* (San Francisco: Harper & Row, 1987).

34. Ward, trans., *The Sayings of the Desert Fathers*, 83–84.

35. Gregory the Great, *Pastoral Care*, Ancient Christian Writers 11 (Westminster, Md.: Newman, 1950), Part II, 8 (p. 77).

36. See Peter C. Hodgson, *God's Wisdom: Toward a Theology of Education* (Louisville: Westminster John Knox, 1999).

37. Timothy Fry, ed., *RB 1980: The Rule of St. Benedict in Latin and English with Notes* (Collegeville, Minn.: Liturgical, 1981), 165.

38. See Sarah Coakley's essay, "Deepening Practices: Perspectives from Ascetical and Mystical Theology," in *Practicing Theology: Beliefs and Practices in Christian Life*, ed. Miroslav Volf and Dorothy C. Bass (Grand Rapids: Eerdmans, 2002), 87.

39. Martin Buber, "The Education of Character," in *Between Man and Man* (Boston: Beacon, 1926), 116–17.

40. Buber's description of an encounter with God ("face to face") dovetails with the previously mentioned insight of Barbara Brown Taylor, namely that the people of God hunger for an experience *of* God.

41. See Catherine of Siena, *The Dialogue,* trans. Suzanne Noffke (New York: Paulist, 1980), 4.

42. Bernard E. Meland, *Higher Education and the Human Spirit* (Chicago: University of Chicago Press, 1953), chaps. 1–2.

43. Fry, *R. B. 1980*, 201–3.

44. For a full discussion of the important concepts of consolation and desolation, see chap. 4 in this book.

45. Sharon D. Welch, *A Feminist Ethic of Risk* (Minneapolis: Fortress Press, 1990), 19.

46. Hodgson, *God's Wisdom,* 6.

Chapter 4: Formational Voices

1. See Reinhold Niebuhr, *Moral Man and Immoral Society: A Study in Ethics and Politics* (New York: Scribners, 1932); *The Children of Light and the Children of Darkness: A Vindication of Democracy and a Critique of Its Traditional Defence* (New York: Scribners, 1944); *Christian Realism and Political Problems* (New York: Scribners, 1953).

2. See Naomi Burton Stone and Patrick Hart, eds., *Thomas Merton, Love and Living* (New York: Harcourt Brace, 1965).

3. Thich Nhat Hanh, *Creating True Peace: Ending Violence in Yourself, Your Family, Your Community, and the World* (New York: Free Press, 2003); see also Robert Ellsberg, ed., *Thich Nhat Hanh: Essential Writings,* Modern Spiritual Masters Series (Maryknoll, N.Y.: Orbis, 2001).

4. Gordon D. Kaufman, *In Face of Mystery: A Constructive Theology* (Cambridge: Harvard University Press, 1993), 307.

5. Ibid., 80.

6. From Janet Ruffing, "Sevenfold Results in the Direction Relationship that Signifies the Work of the Holy Spirit" (Paper delivered at the Annual Conference of Spiritual Directors International, 1994).

7. Timothy Fry, ed., *RB 1980: The Rule of St. Benedict in Latin and English with Notes* (Collegeville, Minn.: Liturgical, 1981), 157.

8. Esther de Waal, *Seeking God: The Way of St. Benedict* (Collegeville, Minn.: Liturgical, 1984), 41.

9. Fry, *RB 1980*, 157.

10. For Benedict the exhortation to *listening* was also inextricably linked with a monk's obedience to the abbot.

11. de Waal, *Seeking God*, 43.

12. Ibid.

13. Ibid.

14. Francis K. Nemeck and Marie T. Coombs, *The Way of Spiritual Direction* (Collegeville, Minn.: Liturgical, 1985), 34.

15. George A. Panichas, ed., *Simone Weil* (Wakefield, R.I.: Moyer Bell, 1977), 44–52.

16. Cited in ibid., 17–18.

17. For guidelines toward a group process of *lectio divina*, see appendix.

18. See my essay, "August in Her Breast: Prayer as Embodiment," in *Setting the Table: Women in Theological Conversation*, Rita Nakashima Brock, Claudia Camp, and Serene Jones, eds. (St. Louis: Chalice, 1995), 205–18.

19. Carolyn Gratton, *The Art of Spiritual Guidance: A Contemporary Approach to Growing in the Spirit* (New York: Crossroad, 1995), 7.

20. Ibid., 8.

21. Merton, "Learning to Live," in Stone and Hart, *Love and Living*, 3.

22. Walter Brueggemann, "Covenanting as Human Vocation," *Interpretation* 33 (1979): 126.

23. Ronald A. Heifetz, *Leadership Without Easy Answers* (Cambridge: Belknap of Harvard University Press, 1999), 14–15.

24. See Alan M. Fairweather, ed., *Nature and Grace: Selections from the Summa Theologica of Thomas Aquinas*, Library of Christian Classics 11 (Philadelphia: Westminster, 1954), 198, 214–15.

25. Robert Kegan, *In Over Our Heads: The Mental Demands of Modern Life* (Cambridge: Harvard University Press, 1994), 164.

26. Brueggemann, "Covenanting," 126.

27. Gratton, *The Art of Spiritual Guidance*, 157.

28. Ibid.

29. See ibid., 160–61.

30. Merton, "Learning to Live," cited in Stone and Hart, *Love and Living*, 3.

31. Gratton, *The Art of Spiritual Guidance*, 158.

32. Augustine, *In Evangelium Iohannis tractatus*, 80.3, in Radbodus Willems, ed., *Sancti Aurelii Augustini in Iohannis Evangelium tractatus* CXXIV, Corpus Christianorum 36 (Turnhout [Belgium]: Brepols, 1954), 529.

33. Jerome, *Commentarioli in Psalmos*, cited in Louis-Marie Chauvet, *The Sacraments: The Word of God at the Mercy of the Body*, trans. Madeleine Beaumont (Collegeville, Minn.: Liturgical, 2001), 43.

34. Dawn DeVries, *Jesus Christ in the Preaching of Calvin and Schleiermacher* (Louisville: Westminster John Knox, 1996), 17.

35. Cited in Edmund Colledge and Bernard McGinn, trans., *Meister Eckhart: The Essential Sermons, Commentaries, Treatises, and Defense*, Classics of Western Spirituality (New York: Paulist, 1981), 250.

36. Fry. *RB 1980*, 229.

37. For an earlier version of this and the following few paragraphs, see my "August in Her Breast," 206–08.

38. James Carroll, *Contemplation* (New York: Paulist, 1979), 26.

39. Teresa of Avila, *The Life of Teresa of Avila*, trans. and ed. E. Allison Peers (New York: Doubleday, 1960), VII, 102.

40. Macrina Wiederkehr, *A Tree Full of Angels: Seeing the Holy in the Ordinary* (San Francisco: HarperCollins, 1988), xii.

41. Teresa of Avila, *The Life*, VIII, 109.

42. Teresa of Avila, *The Interior Castle*, Classics of Western Spirituality, trans. Kieran Kavanaugh and Otilio Rodriguez (New York: Paulist, 1979), 106.

43. See Julian of Norwich, *Showings*, trans. Edmund Colledge and James Walsh, Classics of Western Spirituality (New York: Paulist, 1978), 186.

44. Thich Nhat Hanh, *The Miracle of Mindfulness: A Manual on Meditation* (Boston: Beacon, 1987), 23.

45. Hannah Arendt, *The Human Condition* (Chicago: University of Chicago Press, 1958), 9.

46. Douglas John Hall and Rosemary Radford Ruether, *God and the Nations*, The Hein-Fry Lectures (Minneapolis: Fortress Press, 1995), 26–27.

47. Dorothy Day, *The Autobiography of Dorothy Day* (New York: Harper & Row, 1952), 44.

48. See David Tracy, *The Analogical Imagination: Christian Theology and the Culture of Pluralism* (New York: Crossroad, 1981).

CHAPTER 5: MENDING THE GAPS

1. See Gerald May, *Will and Spirit* (New York: Harper & Row, 1982), 163–64.

2. Carolyn Gratton, *The Art of Spiritual Guidance: A Contemporary Approach to Growing in the Spirit* (New York: Crossroad, 1995), 23.

3. See Parker J. Palmer, "Action and Contemplation: A Living Paradox," in *The Active Life: A Spirituality of Work, Creativity, and Caring* (San Francisco: HarperSanFrancisco, 1990), 15–35.

4. Gratton, *The Art of Spiritual Guidance*, 7.

5. Thomas Merton, "Creative Silence," in Naomi Burton Stone and Patrick Hart, eds., *Thomas Merton, Love and Living* (New York: Harcourt Brace, 1965), 39.

6. In North American churches that are *thriving*, however, there has been a renaissance of receptive practices. See Diana Butler Bass, *The Practicing Congregation: Imagining a New Old Church* (Herndon, Va.: Alban Institute, 2004).

7. Merton, "Creative Silence," in Stone and Hart, *Love and Living*, 41.

8. John K. Galbraith, *The Affluent Society* (Boston: Houghton Mifflin, 1998), 125.

9. Juliet Schor, *The Overworked American: The Unexpected Decline of Leisure* (New York: Basic, 1991), 126.

10. Palmer, *Active Life*, 39.

11. See appendix for a full description of group *lectio divina*.

12. Palmer, *Active Life*, 122–23.

13. Teresa of Avila, *The Life of Teresa of Avila*, trans. and ed. E. Allison Peers (New York: Doubleday, 1960), XL, 394.

14. Margaret Silf, *Inner Compass: An Invitation to Ignatian Spirituality* (Chicago: Jesuit Way/Loyola Press, 1999), 52–53.

15. Ibid., 53.

16. Spiritual guide Ignatius of Loyola urged his followers to make a review of their lives each day—even if it was the only prayer of the day, to monitor consolation and desolation. Some spiritual directors call this practice a "review of conscience," and others "a review of consciousness." Ignatius called it an *examen*. The *examen* has five parts: (1) gratitude for God and for the specific "gifts" through which God's presence has been felt throughout the day; (2) asking for help in seeking to see God more clearly, love God more dearly; (3) recollecting the many ways we have missed God's presence and consequently failed to *reflect* God's presence throughout the day; (4) a movement interiorly to simply resting in God; (5) a recommitment to be more sensitive to God's love and quick to receive God's grace. Daily repetition of this prayer develops a quick recognition of consolation (typically when we are living from our deepest desires and God's intentions for our lives) and desolation (when we are living under the pressure of others' expectations of us, or to our own egocentric and misleading desires).

17. Larry Dossey, *Prayer Is Good Medicine: How to Reap the Healing Benefits of Prayer* (San Francisco: HarperSanFrancisco, 1996), 2–6.

18. Ibid., 5.

19. Ibid., 59.

20. Reinhold Niebuhr, *Nature and Destiny of Man* (New York: Scribners, 1948); see also chaps. 2 and 4.

21. Katherine M. Dyckman, Mary Garvin, and Elizabeth Liebert, *The Spiritual Exercises Reclaimed: Uncovering Liberating Possibilities for Women* (New York: Paulist, 2001), 102.

22. John J. English, *Spiritual Freedom: From an Experience of the Ignatian Exercises to the Art of Spiritual Guidance* (Chicago: Loyola, 1995), 37–38.

23. David L. Fleming, *Draw Me into Your Friendship: A Literal Translation and Contemporary Reading of the Spiritual Exercises* (St. Louis: Institute of Jesuit Sources, 1996), paragraph 23, 28–29.

24. Those familiar with Ignatius will recognize "The Two Standards" in which those things "not of God" (namely, honor, riches, and pride) vie with those things that are of Christ (poverty, service, and humility). See ibid., paragraphs 136–48, 110–15.

25. May, *Will and Spirit*, 226–27.

26. Jane E. Vennard, "The Compassionate Observer," *Presence: The Journal of Spiritual Directors International* 4, no. 3 (September 1998): 28.

27. Ibid., 33.

CHAPTER 6: FORMATIONAL SERMONS

1. Because—and in honor of—the unnamed woman in Mark 14:9 this note is in honor of my amazing mother, Thelma Ann Northcutt (July 20, 1935–April 20, 1999).

2. Thanks to Leah Phillips, who employed this amazing list of acronyms for the Offering Meditation at First Christian Church, Stillwater, Oklahoma; Senior Sunday, May 6, 2004.

3. Walter Brueggemann, "Covenanting as Human Vocation," *Interpretation* 33 (1979): 115–29.

4. Linda Grant, "Checking the Checkpoints," *Guardian*, February 2, 2004.

5. Hannah Arendt, *The Human Condition* (Chicago: University of Chicago Press, 1958), 9: "The new beginning inherent makes itself felt in the world—through the capacity of beginning something new."

6. Julian Bond, remarks from an evening sponsored by The University of Tulsa's Law School; Spring, 2003.

7. Anahad O'Connor, "Why Some Prison Guards Have Refused to Join in the Abuse: Psychology Offers Clues," *New York Times* International Edition, May 14, 2004.

8. Douglas John Hall and Rosemary Radford Ruether, *God and the Nations*, Hein-Fry Lectures (Minneapolis: Fortress Press, 1995), 26–27.

9. Amanda Paulsell Madigan is my goddaughter. I received permission from her mother to re-tell this story from Amanda's life.

10. James M. Clark and John V. Skinner, *Treatises and Sermons of Meister Eckhart* (New York: Harper & Bros., 1958), 194.

11. William B. Silverman, *Rabbinic Stories for Christian Ministers and Teachers* (Nashville: Abingdon, 1958), 75.

12. Suzanne F. Singer, "Hi-tech Tools Reconstruct Umm el-Kanatir," *Biblical Archaeology Review* 33, no. 6 (November/December 2007): 53–60, 86.

APPENDIX 1: SERMON PREPARATION

1. Thomas H. Troeger, *Imagining a Sermon* (Nashville: Abingdon, 1990).

2. See chapter 5 for discussion of these interdependent pairs.

3. Several of my students who have utilized this exegetical guide for years in their weekly sermon preparation, advise me that *sometimes* when a sermon is "stuck"—even after weeding the garden—an ideal "life-line" at this point of sermon preparation is a conversation with a colleague or a peer in ministry.

APPENDIX 2: *LECTIO DIVINA*

1. Guigo II, *The Ladder of Monks: A Letter on the Contemplative Life and Twelve Meditations,* trans. with an introduction by Edmund Colledge and James Walsh, Cistercian Studies Series 48 (Kalamazoo, Mich.: Cistercian Publications, 1981). Guigo's system had four parts: reading, meditation, prayer, and contemplation.

2. See Paul Ricoeur, *The Symbolism of Evil* (New York: Harper & Row, 1967).

3. See Teresa of Avila, *The Interior Castle, Classics of Western Spirituality,* trans. Kieran Kavanaugh and Otilio Rodriguez (New York: Paulist, 1979), 6, 7, 10.

INDEX

Ignatius of Loyola, xii, 38, 83, 109–10, 112–14, 140
Irenaeus of Lyons, 27, 34, 55
Jerome, 93
Jesus, xii, 4, 6, 7, 9, 10, 24, 25, 26, 34, 36, 53, 55, 60, 63, 67, 70, 73, 79, 80, 92, 106–7, 123, 127, 134–36, 143
Jeter, Joseph R., Jr., xii
Johnson, Elizabeth, 7
Johnson, Jerry, 28–29, 31, 35–36
Julian of Norwich, 49, 95
Kaufman, Gordon, 6, 80, 81, 83
Kegan, Robert, 89
King, Martin Luther, Jr., 28, 36, 51, 121
Lectio divina, 8, 84, 85, 102, 105, 107, 139–40, 145–47
Linn, Edmund, 42
Lischer, Richard, 18
Listening, 3, 4, 19, 56–57, 76, 81–84, 87, 105, 112, 125–31
Long, Thomas G., 15, 16, 33, 46
Lowry, Eugene, 16
Luther, Martin, 70, 77
Mahan, Brian, 71
Mandela, Nelson, 6
Marcel, Gabriel, 14–15, 24, 25
May, Gerald, 65, 104, 113
McClure, John, 19
McKnight, John, 48
Meland, Bernard, 76–77
Merton, Thomas, 38, 51, 56, 70, 72–73, 79, 88–91, 92, 97, 105
Meister Eckhart, 1, 94, 131, 133
Miles, Margaret, 24–25, 27, 65
Mountford, Roxanne, 39, 64
Nemeck, Francis, 85–86

New Homiletic, the, 16–17
Niebuhr, Reinhold, 45, 47, 79, 112–13
Padovano, Anthony, 60
Paideuterion/a, 3, 58, 61, 74–78, 80, 81, 84, 86
Paidia, 29, 54, 80
Palmer, Parker, 38, 51, 104, 106, 107
Peterson, Eugene, 18
Phelps, Austin, 39, 62
Pittman, Nancy, 62
Plato, 25
Pneuma, 1
Prayer, 3, 5, 6, 10, 19, 28, 29, 30, 32, 38, 52, 57, 58, 64–65, 67–68, 75, 83–84, 85, 89, 92, 94, 95, 97, 106–7, 112, 139–41
    mental, 28, 105
    vocal, 105
    contemplative, 107
Preacher as God person, viii, 13, 15, 26, 29, 64, 68, 89
Preacher as spiritual director, viii, ix, 74, 81, 84, 87–99, 101
Preacher's interior life, vii, 2, 10, 13, 15, 73, 101, 107, 109, 114–15
Preaching as spiritual direction, 13–14, 17, 27, 31–34, 36, 57–58, 60–63, 73, 81–83, 97–99, 111, 114, 139–44
Rahner, Karl, 20, 25, 27, 126
Ruffing, Janet, 65, 86
Ruah, 1
Receptivity, 13–15, 18, 20–23, 26, 29, 55, 61, 72, 74, 75, 86, 93, 103–8, 143
Sacrament/al, viii, 2, 14, 25, 26–29, 93–97, 117, 116, 143
Schor, Juliet, 106

Self-knowledge, 32, 46, 48, 67–73, 75, 82
Self/soul, 52
Shalom, 1, 4, 14, 67, 75
Silf, Margaret, 109–10
Sittler, Joseph, 9–10, 13, 14, 24, 25, 26, 27, 30, 33, 34
Spiritual direction, 3–4, 11, 32, 80–84
    guidance, 1, 7, 8, 13, 33, 34, 59–61, 64, 80–97
    formation, 15, 17, 31–34, 84, 111
    of the preacher/ pastor, 15, 17–20
Spiritual freedom, 72–74
Taylor, Barbara Brown, 36, 60–61, 71–72
Teresa of Avila, xii, 12–13, 22, 28–29, 31, 32, 38, 51–52, 58–60, 68, 69, 71, 79, 94, 95, 108, 125, 126, 131, 146
Teresa of Calcutta, 26, 28–29, 31, 67, 121
Thich Nhat Hanh, 79, 95
Thomas Aquinas, 88
Tillich, Paul, 26, 47
Tracy, David, 5, 7, 51, 75, 97, 98
Troeger, Thomas, 16, 33
Tutu, Desmond, 6
Underhill, Evelyn, 1, 38, 55–56
van Breeman, Peter, 69
Vennard, Jane, 114
Vocational formation, 89–93, 118–31
Ward, Benedicta, 66, 67
Welch, Sharon, 77–78
Weil, Simone, 38, 51, 85–86
Wilkins, John, 62
Wink, Walter, 6
Wright, Wendy, 70